I0762842

CLEVELAND

A KEEPSAKE

Gary J. Sikorski

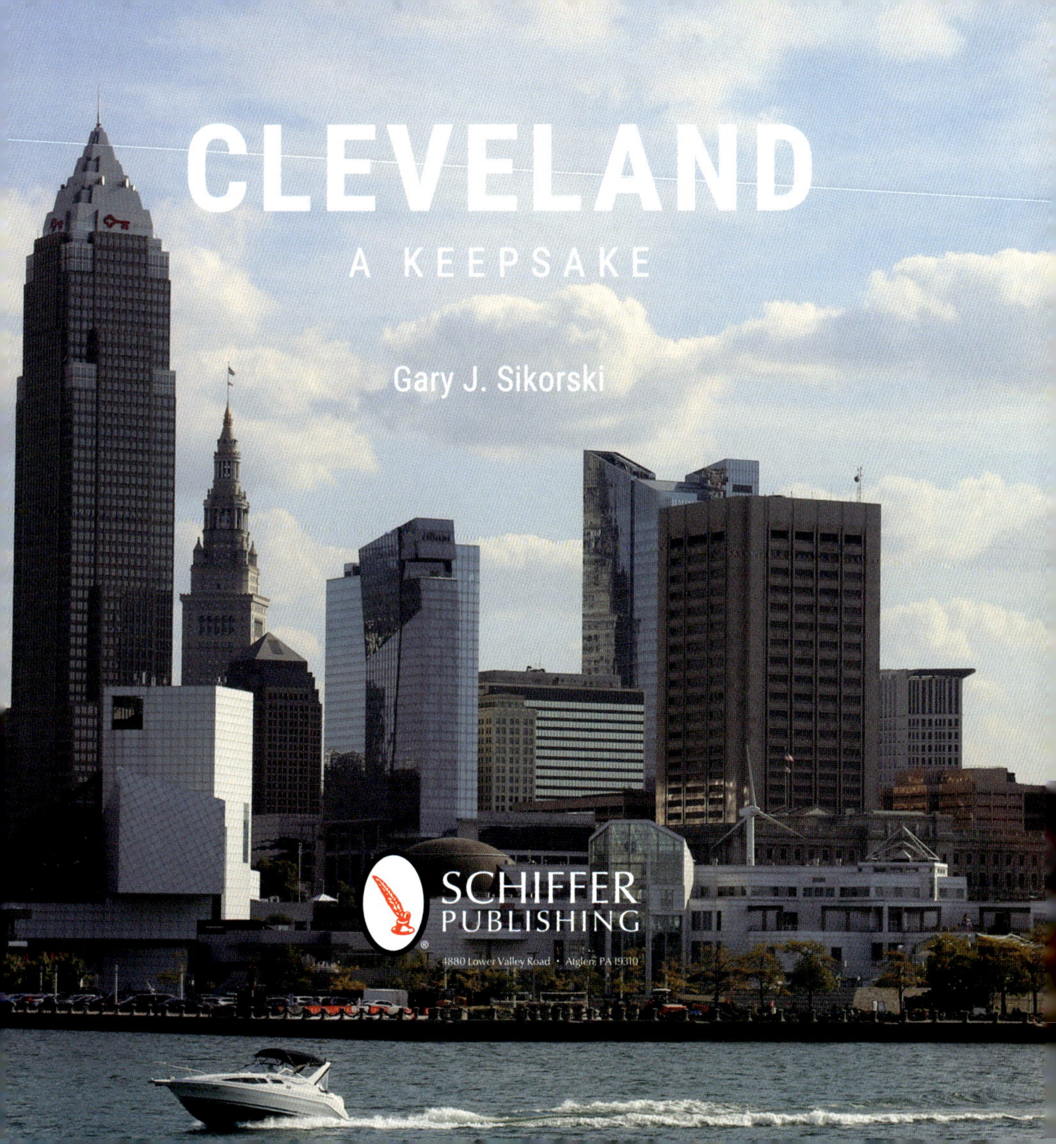

SCHIFFER PUBLISHING
4880 Lower Valley Road • Atglen, PA 19310

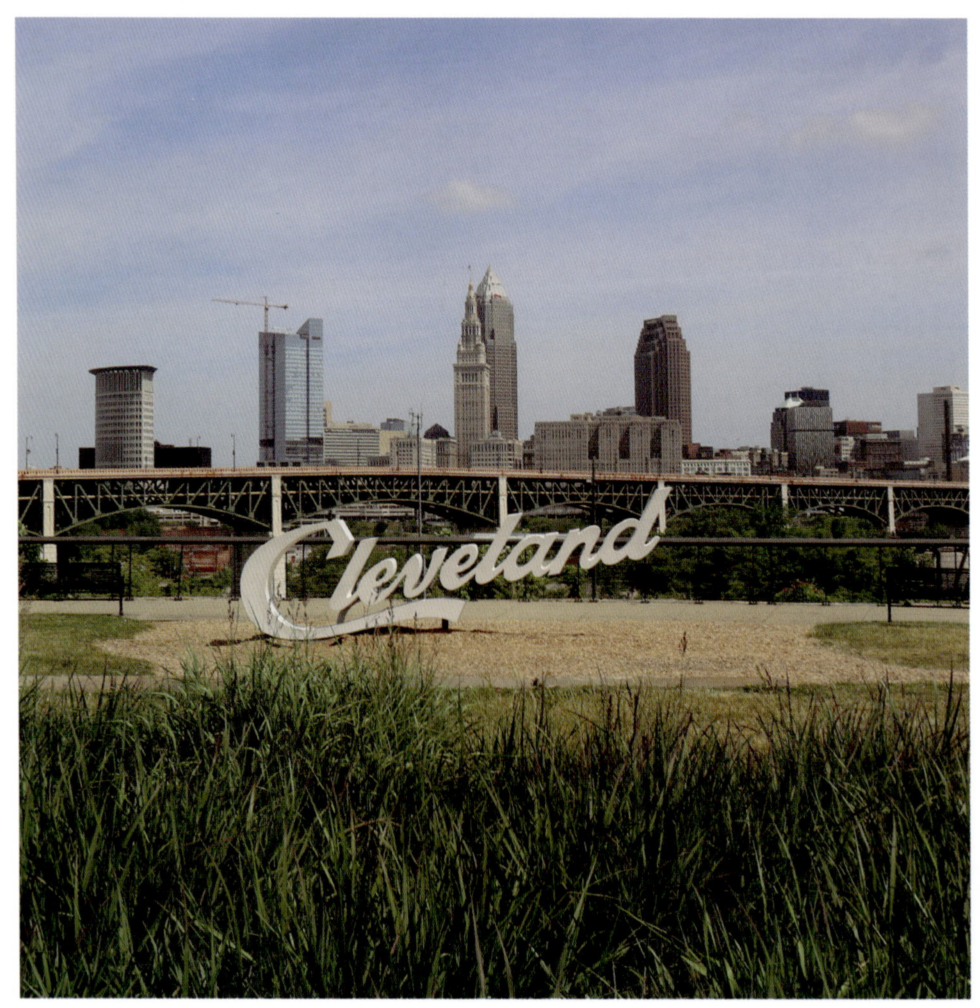

One of the Cleveland Script Signs in Tremont

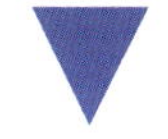

VIEWS OF "THE LAND"

"Life is about the adventures you take and the memories you make."

—Katie Grissom

The city of Cleveland, a port city connected to the Atlantic Ocean via the Saint Lawrence Seaway, was founded in 1796 near the mouth of the Cuyahoga River, in the area known today as the Flats, by the Revolutionary War veteran General Moses Cleaveland. The city's prime geographic location on the river and the lakeshore made it ideal for industrial development, which attracted large numbers of immigrants looking for work and growing the "City on the North Coast" into one of the nation's most successful commercial and industrial centers.

Once a manufacturing hub, Cleveland today finds itself growing into a service-based economy, as well as becoming one of the top travel destinations in the country. The images you'll find on the following pages capture the spirit of this vibrant city, and they will set you on a path toward discovering its wonders. From the Rock & Roll Hall of Fame, to Playhouse Square, to University Circle, down the Cuyahoga River in the Flats, and over to historic Ohio City, "The Land" provides locals and tourists alike with an extraordinary experience.

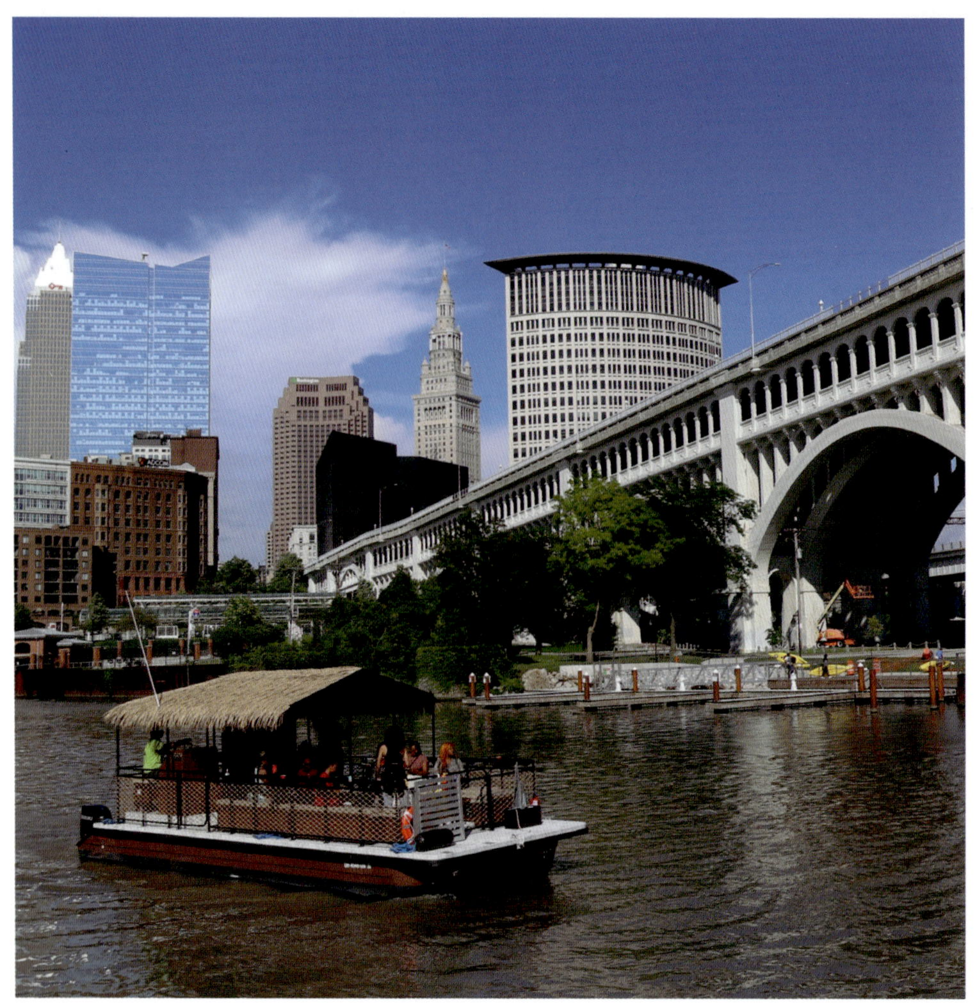

The Cuyahoga River bends past downtown Cleveland.

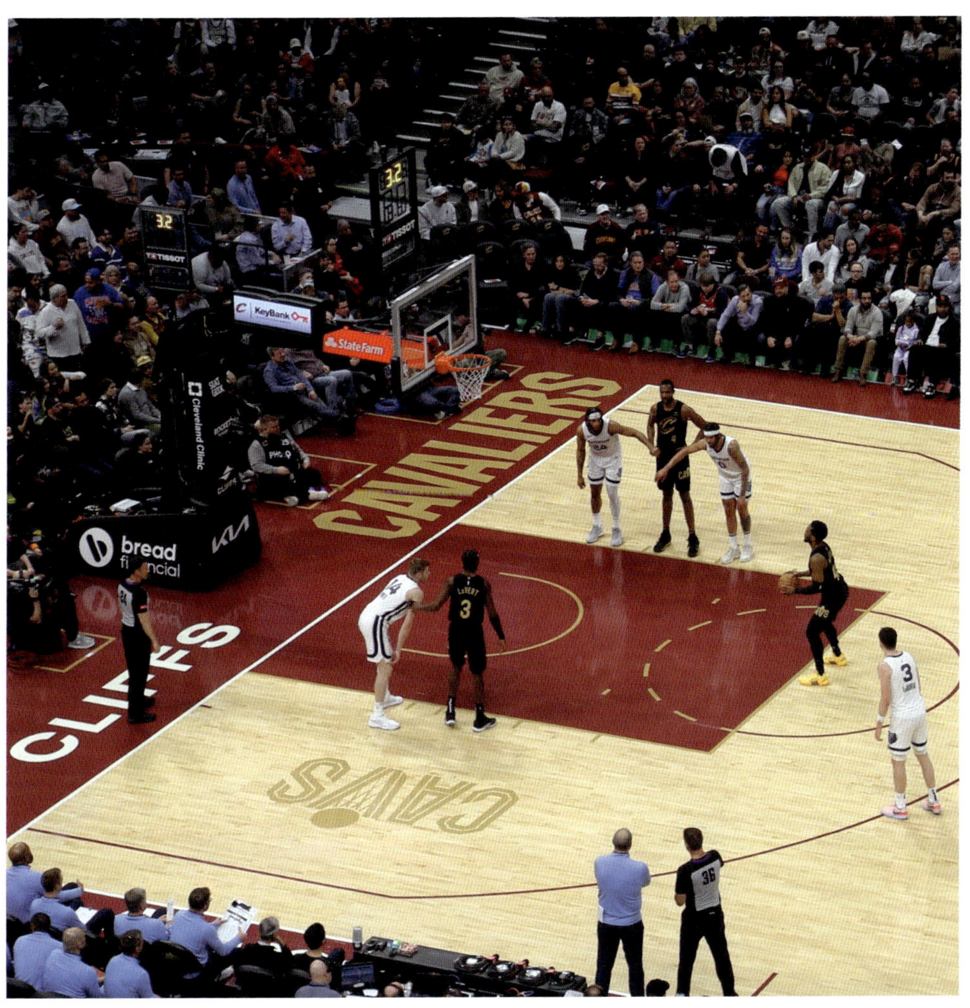

Our Cleveland Cavaliers inside world-class Rocket Arena

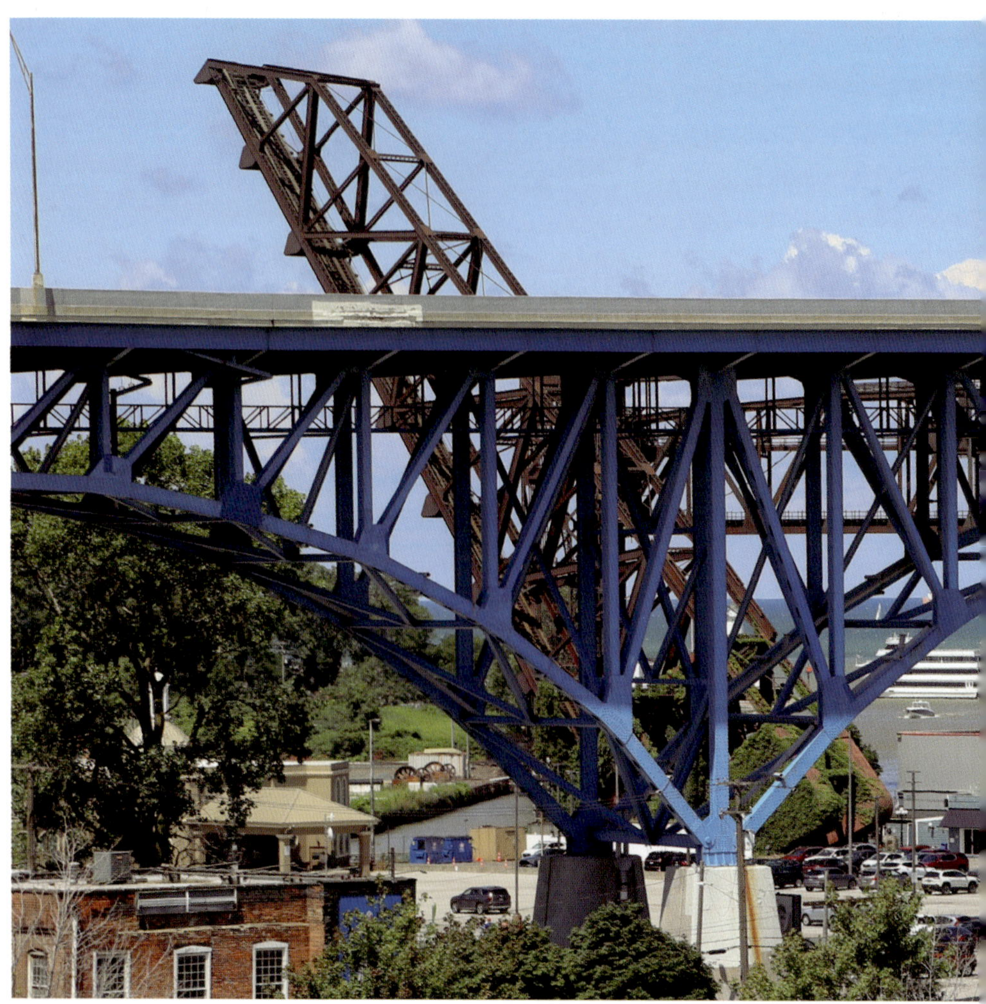

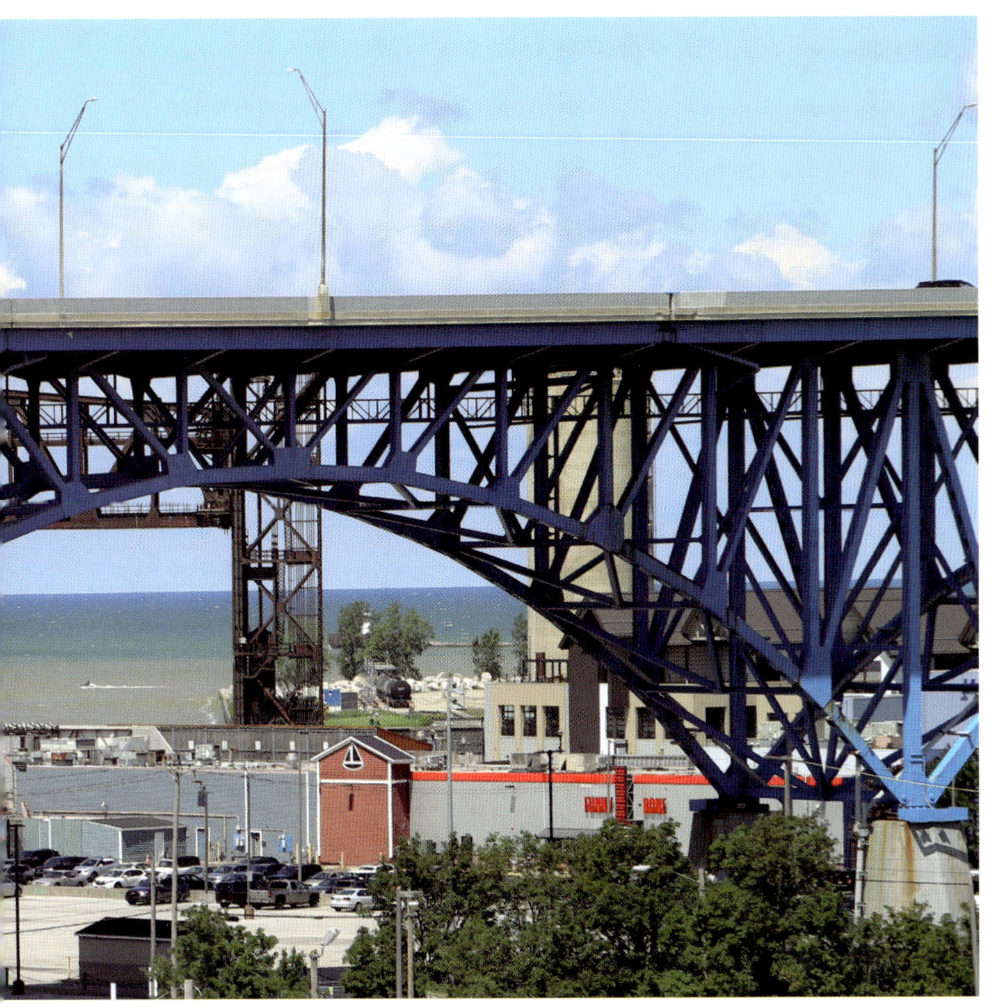

The mouth of the Cuyahoga River under the Main Avenue Bridge

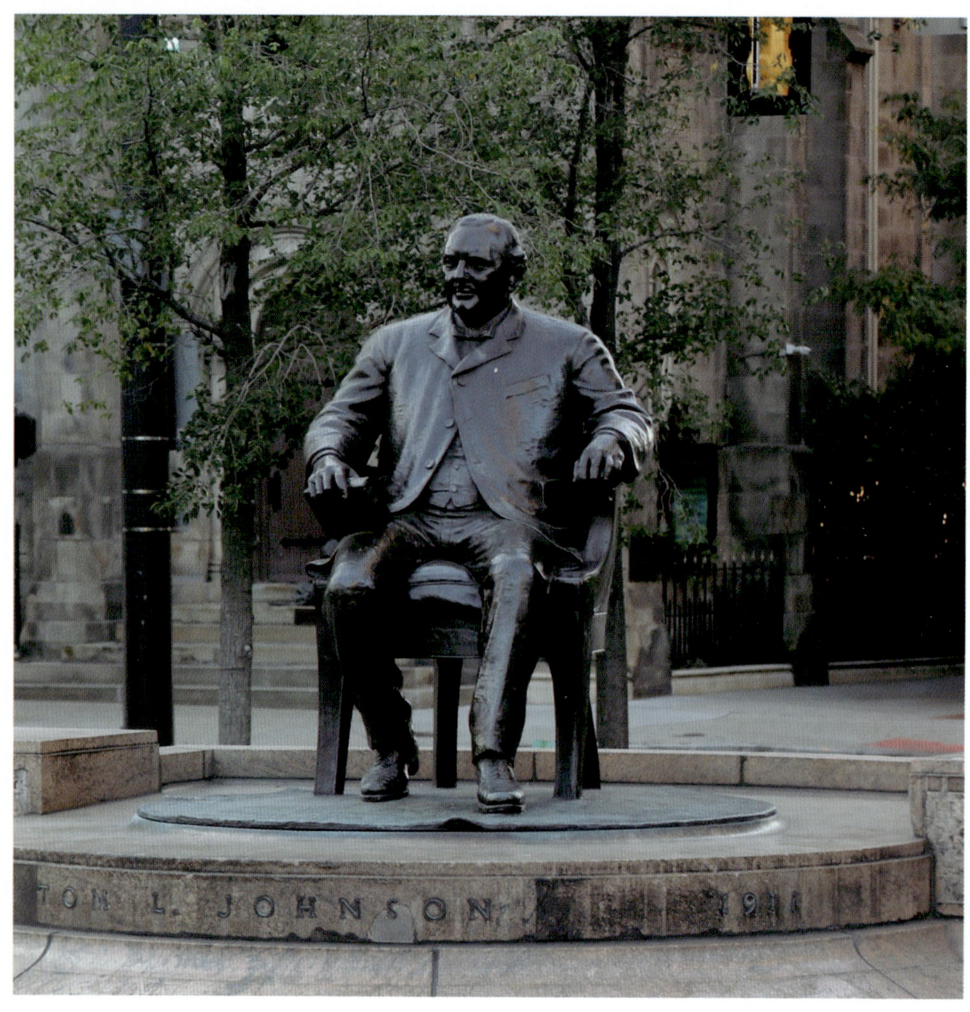

A statue of Tom L. Johnson, Cleveland mayor from 1901 to 1909

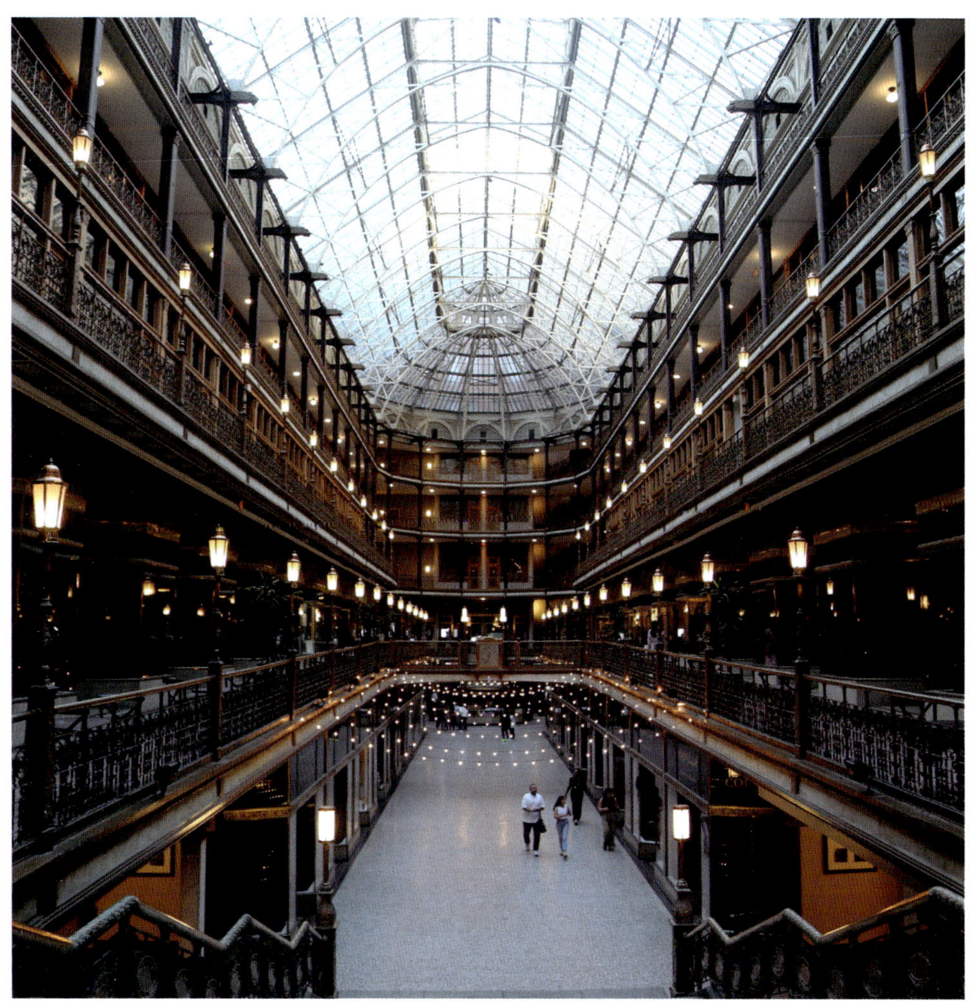

The Arcade Cleveland, America's first indoor shopping center

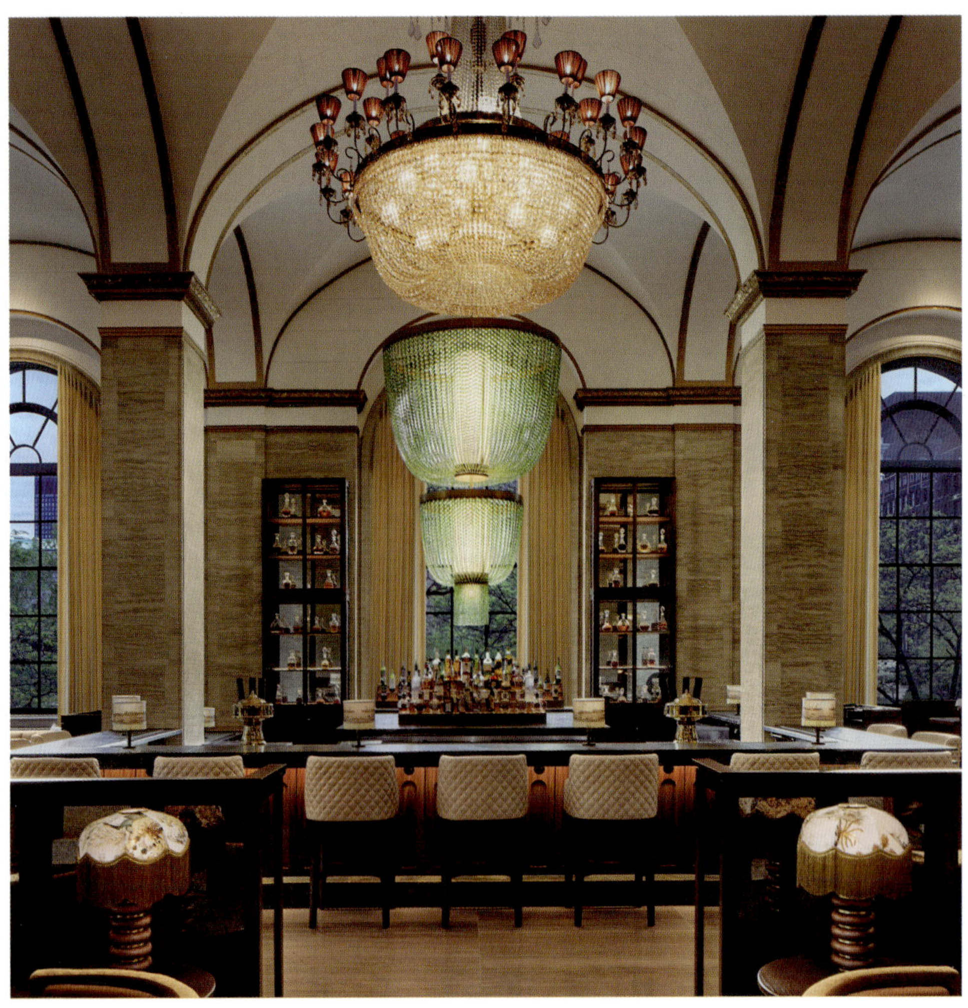

Maker Bar inside the newly renovated Hotel Cleveland

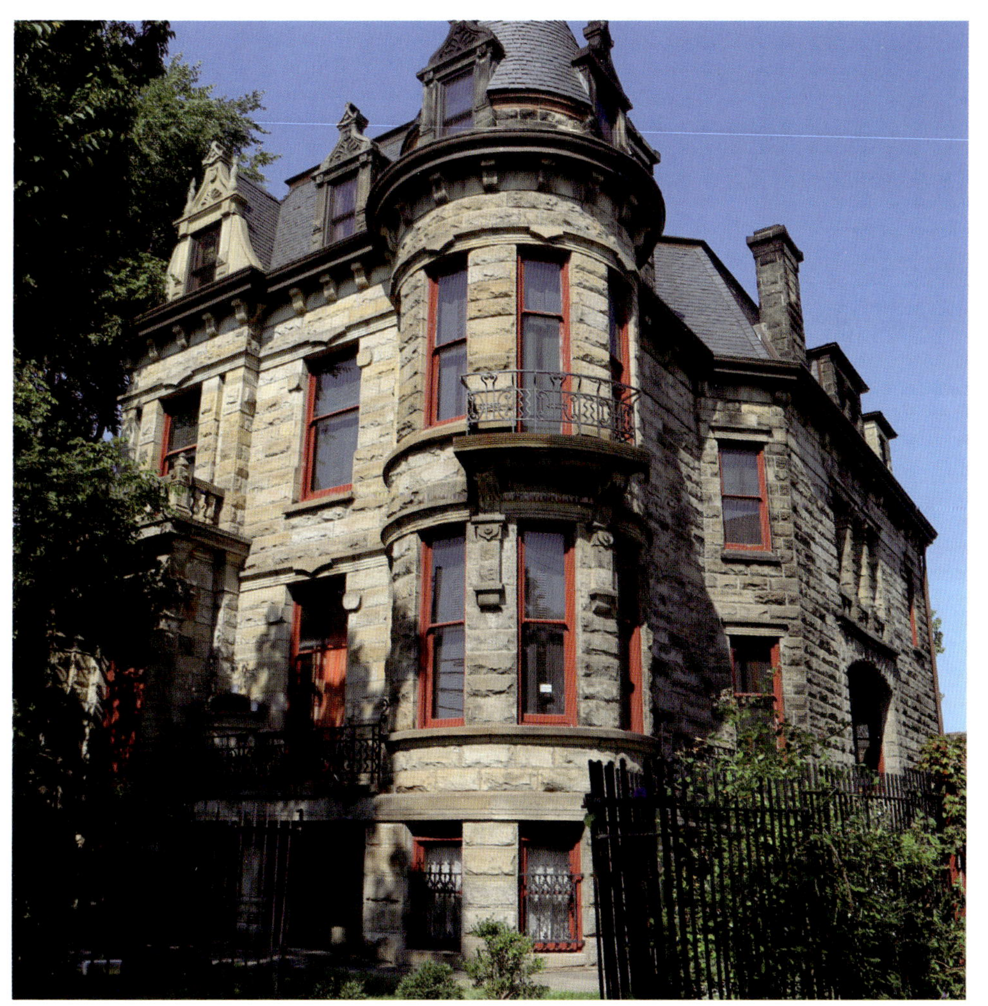

The Franklin Castle is rumored to be haunted.

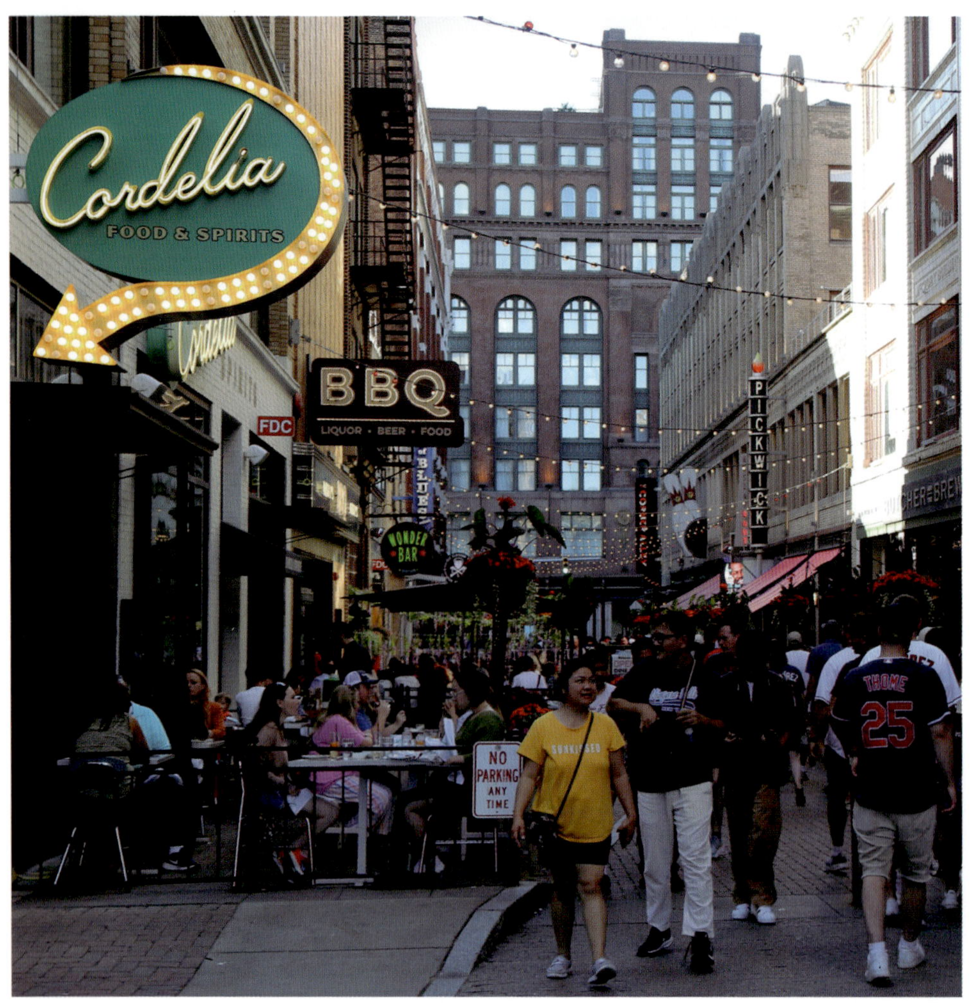

Crowds flock to the restaurants and bars on East 4th Street.

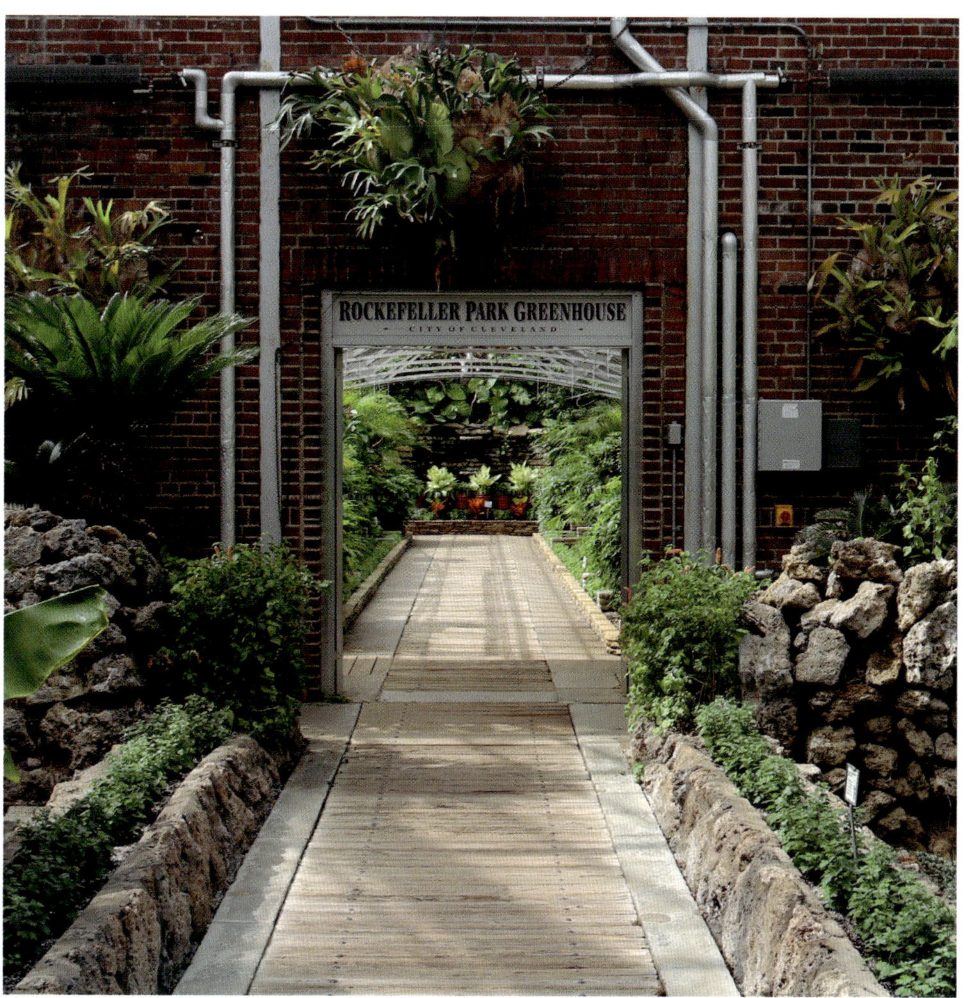

Rockefeller Park Greenhouse

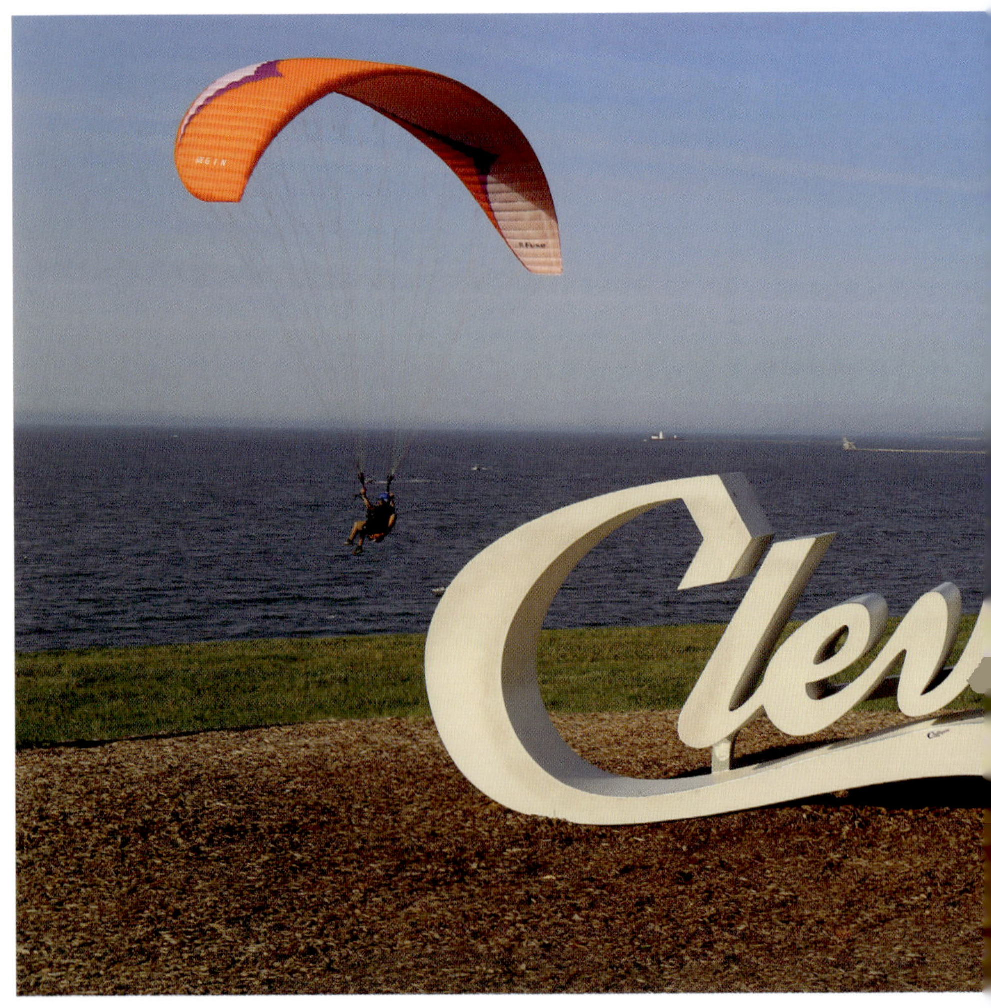

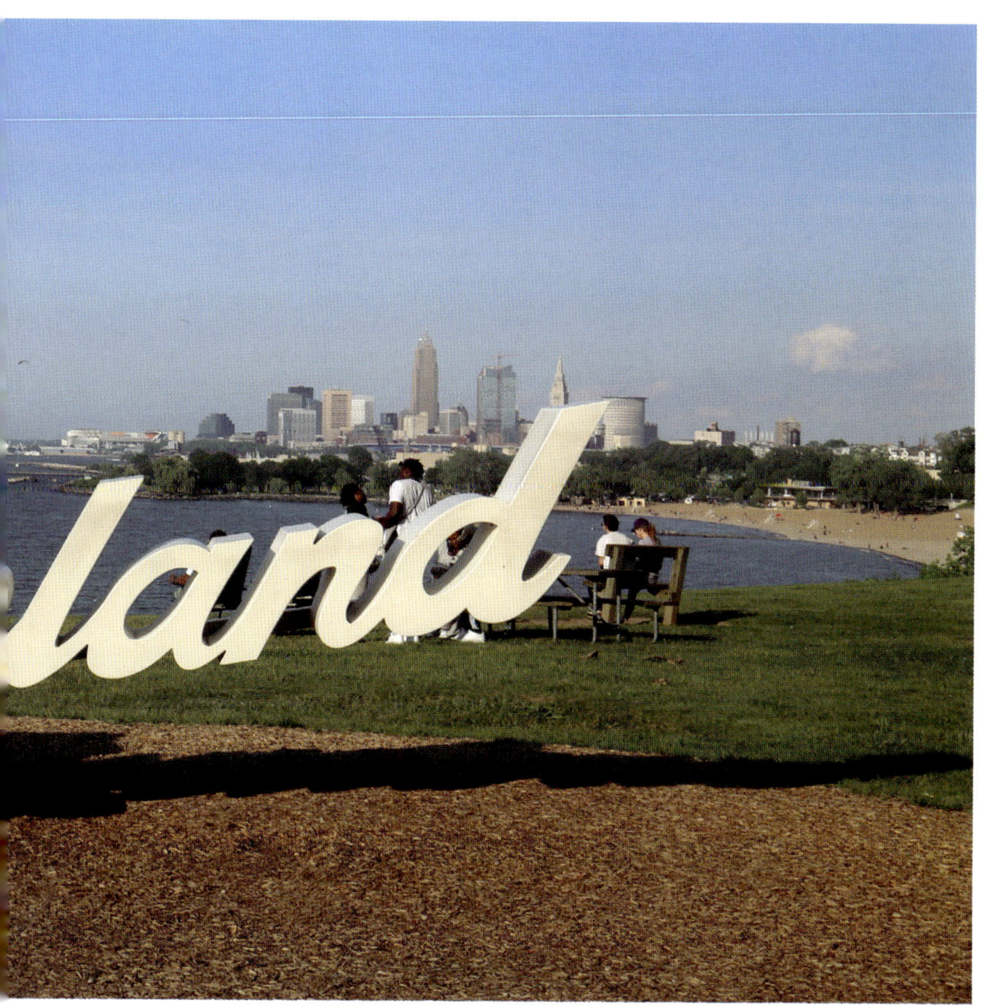

The Cleveland Script Sign in Edgewater Park

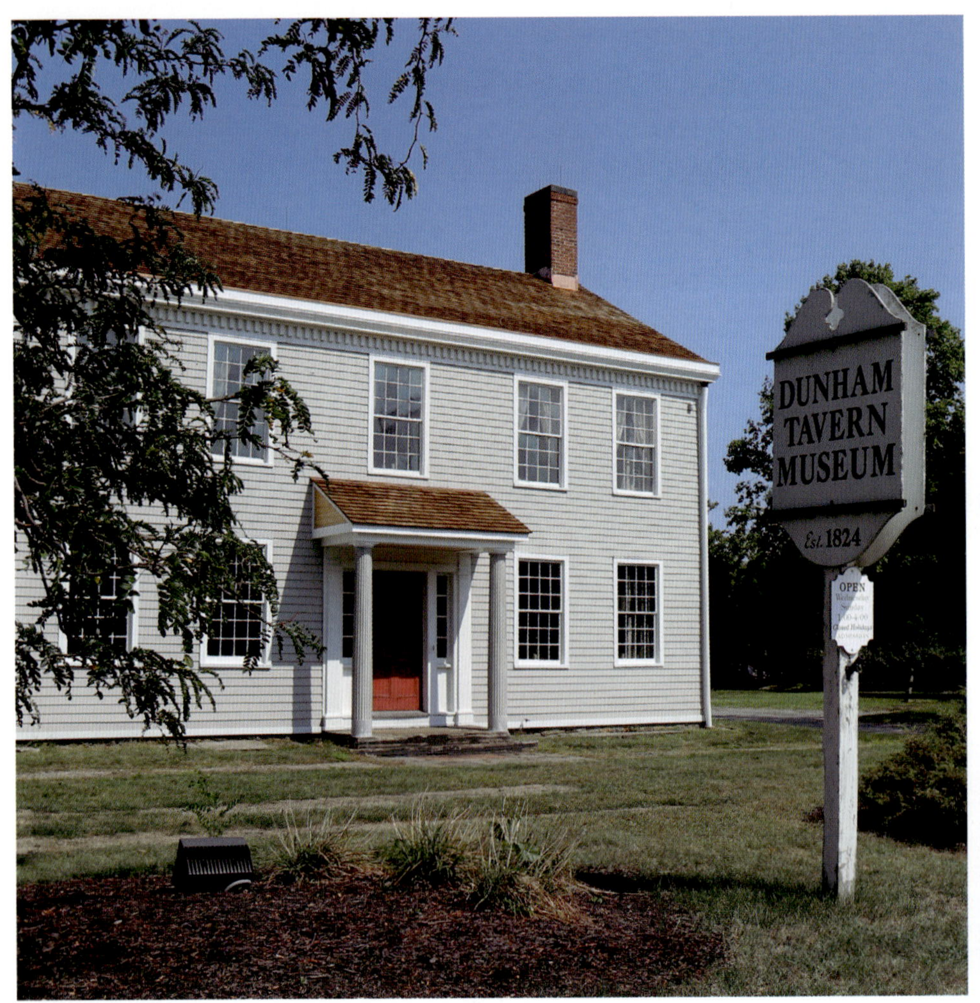

The Dunham Tavern is the oldest building in Cleveland.

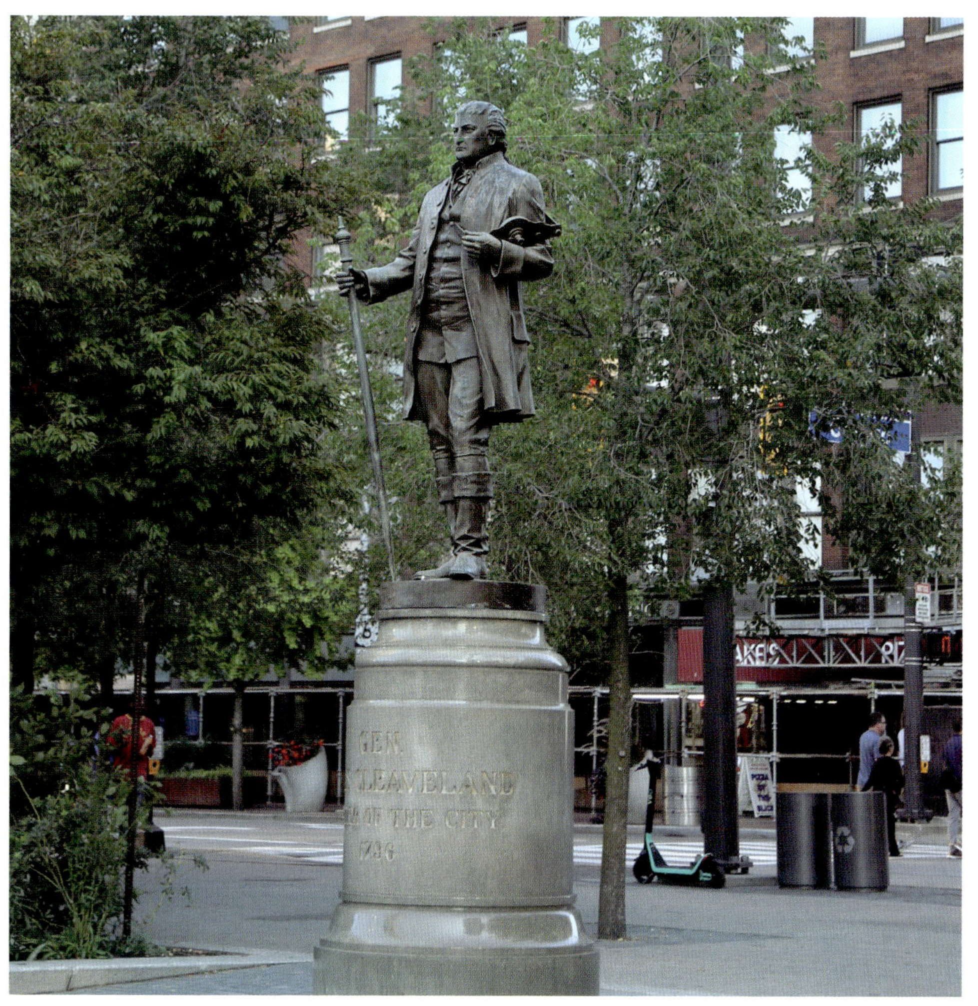

General Moses Cleaveland was the city's founder.

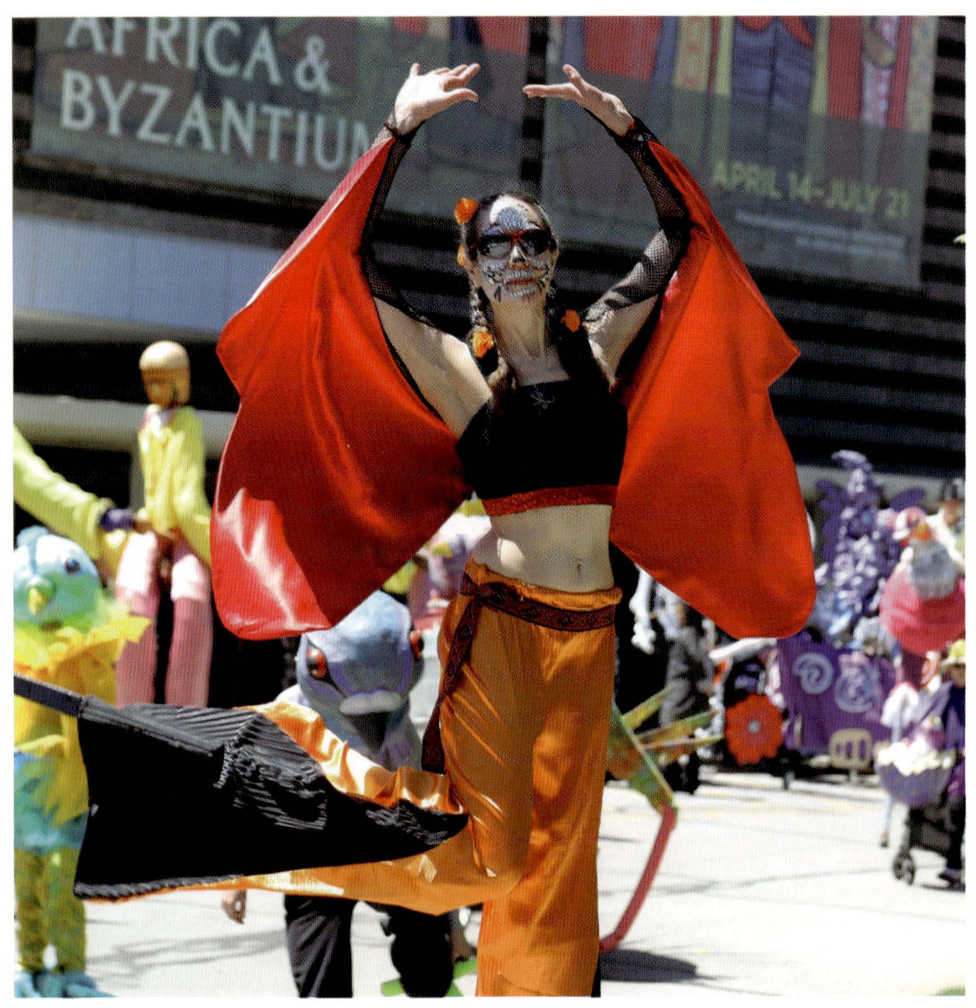

Colorful costumes parade the circle around Wade Oval.

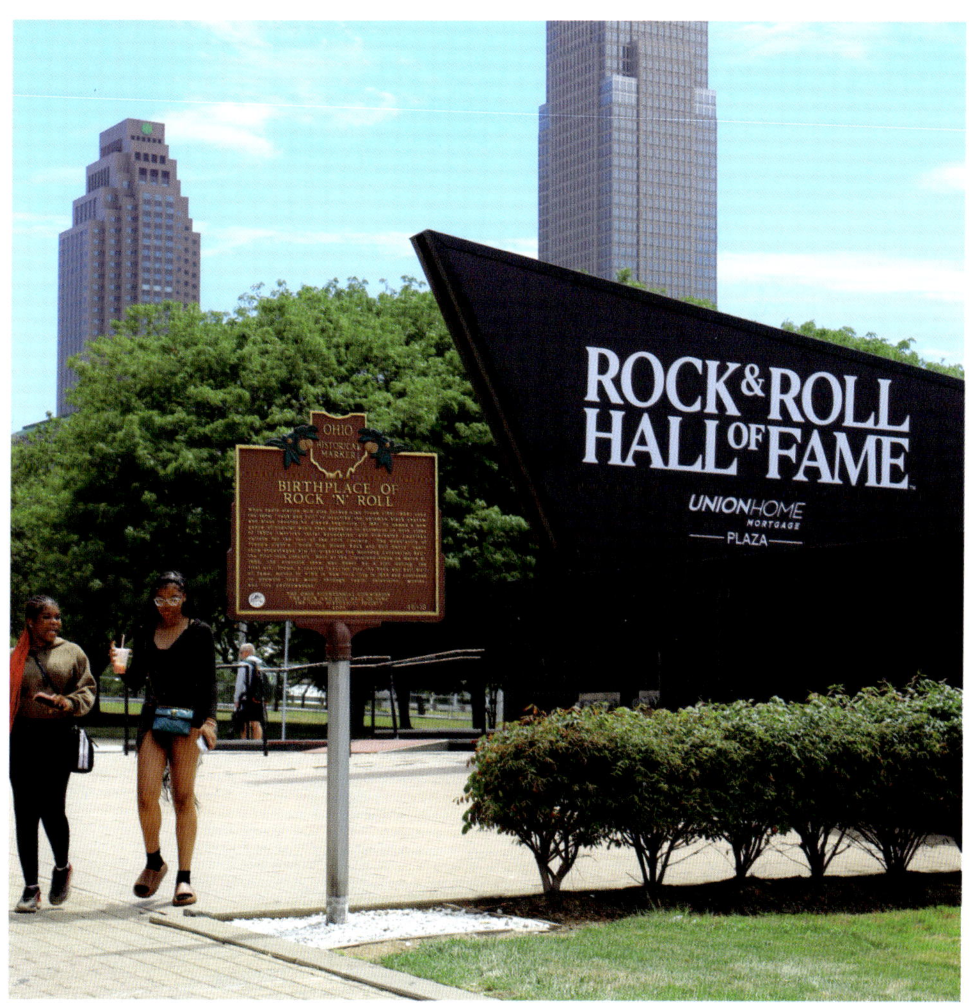

The Rock & Roll Hall of Fame on the East 9th St. Pier

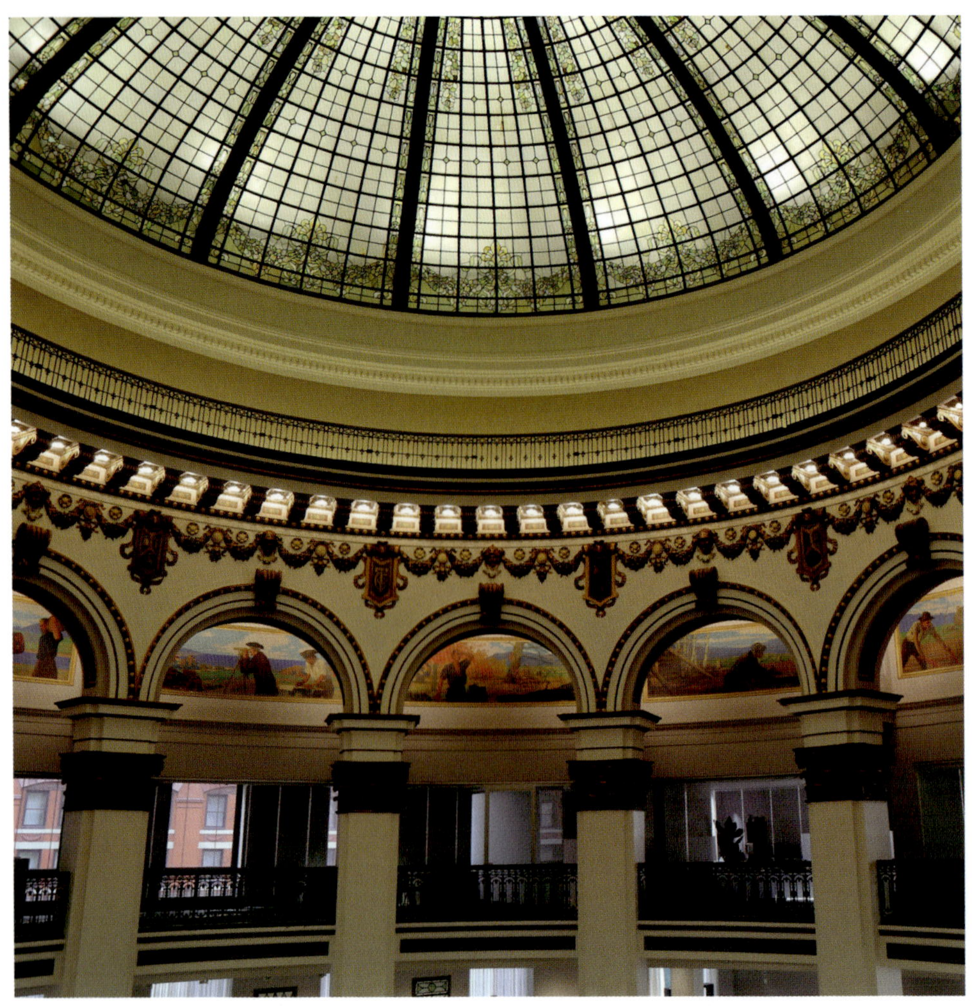

The historic Cleveland Trust Rotunda inside Heinen's Grocery on Euclid Avenue

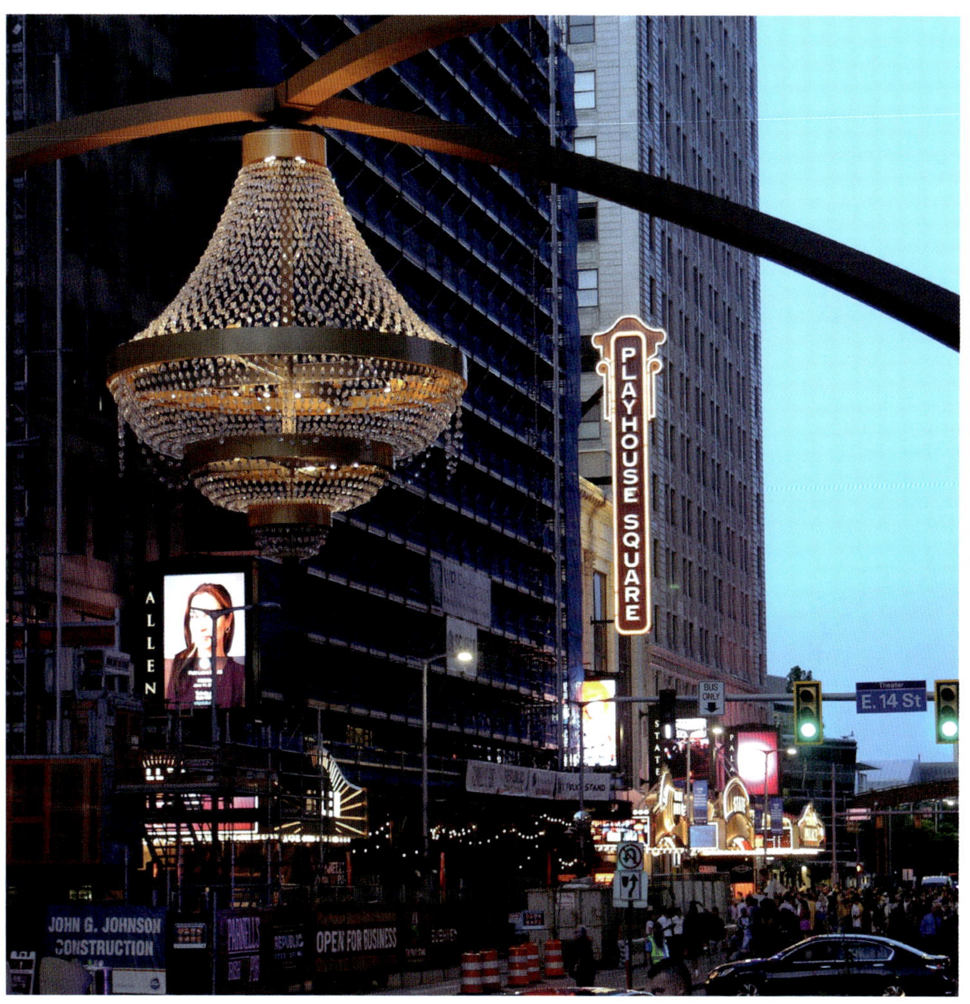

Playhouse Square, the second-largest performing arts center in the country

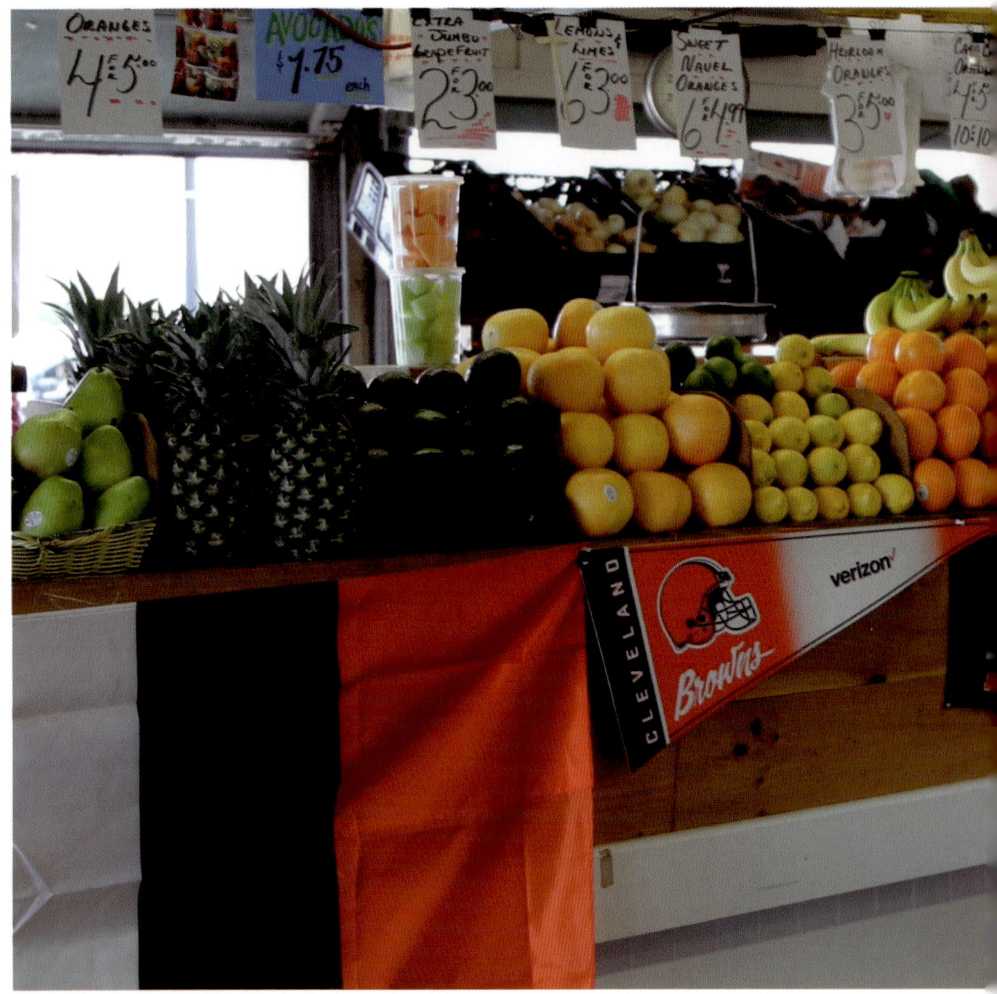
ORANGES
AVOCADOS
$1.75
each
EXTRA JUMBO GRAPEFRUIT
LEMONS & LIMES
SWEET NAVEL ORANGES
HEIRLOOM ORANGES
CLEVELAND
Browns
verizon

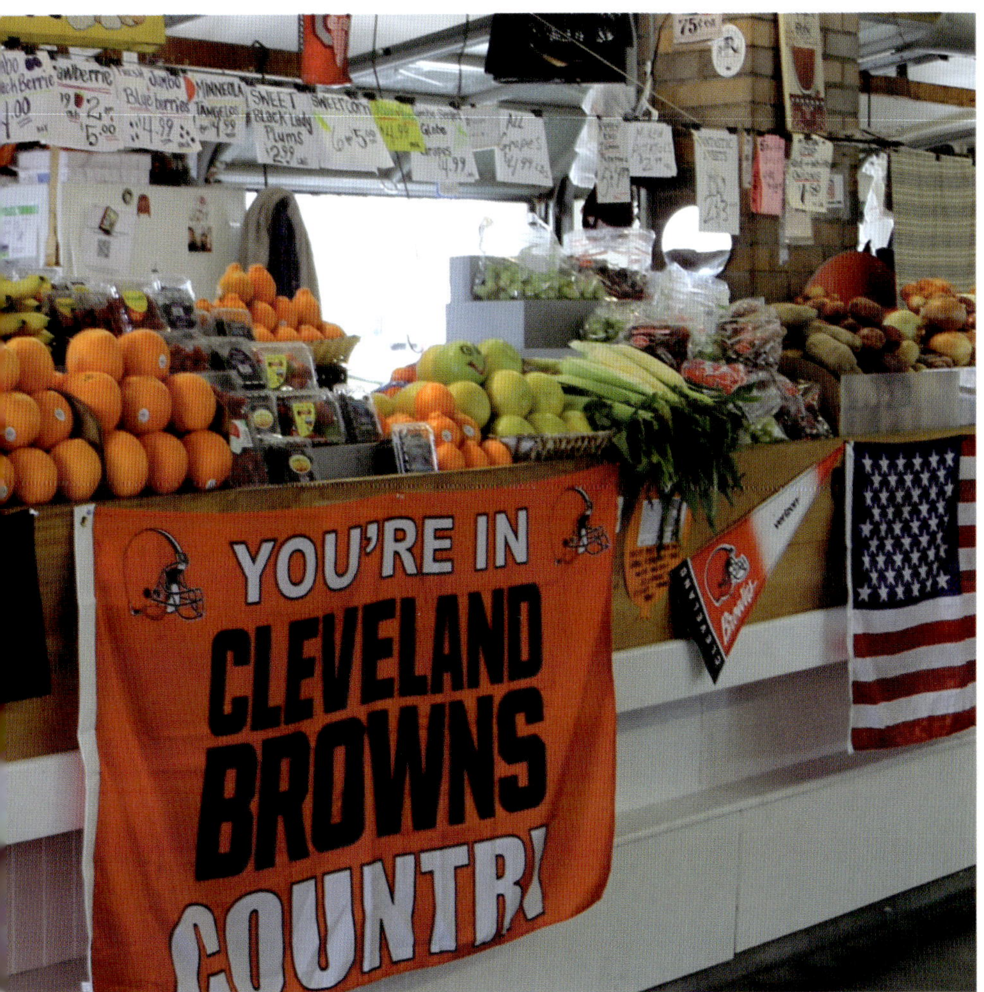

A produce stand at the historic West Side Market

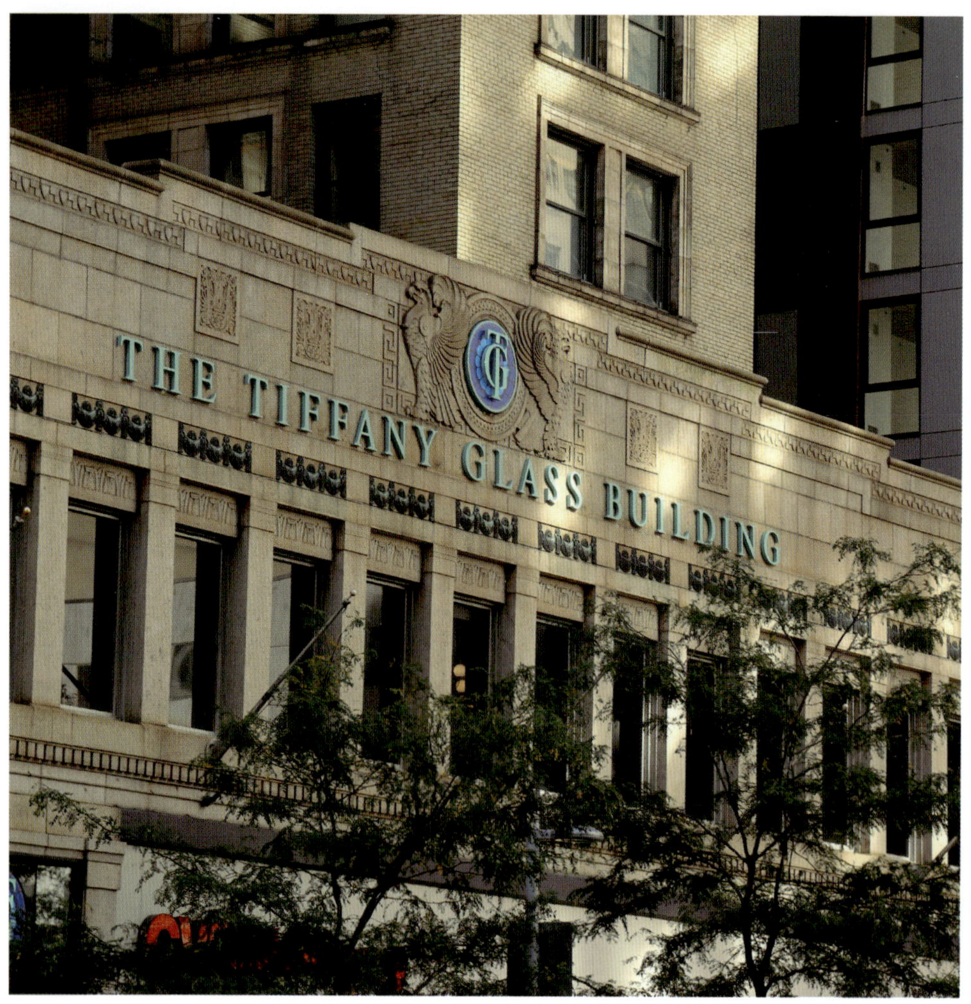

The Tiffany Glass Building on Euclid Avenue

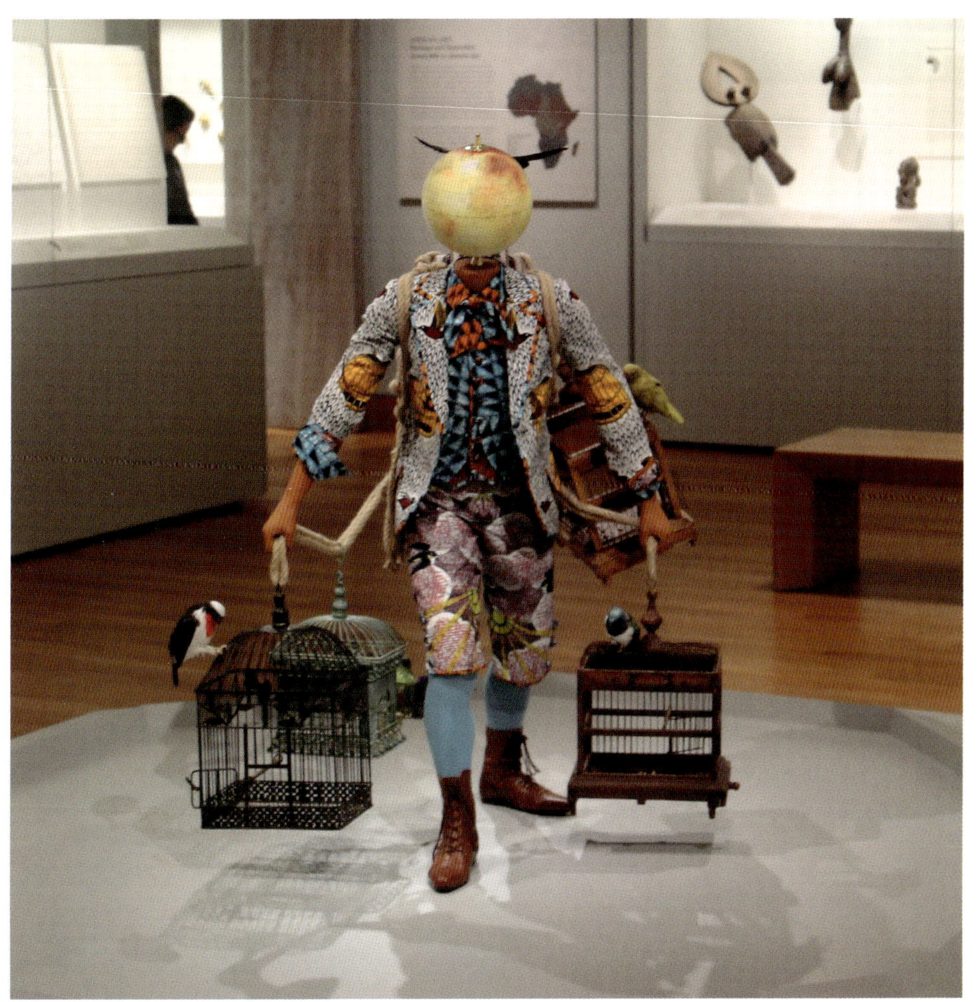

Birdcage Kid (Boy) in the Cleveland Museum of Art

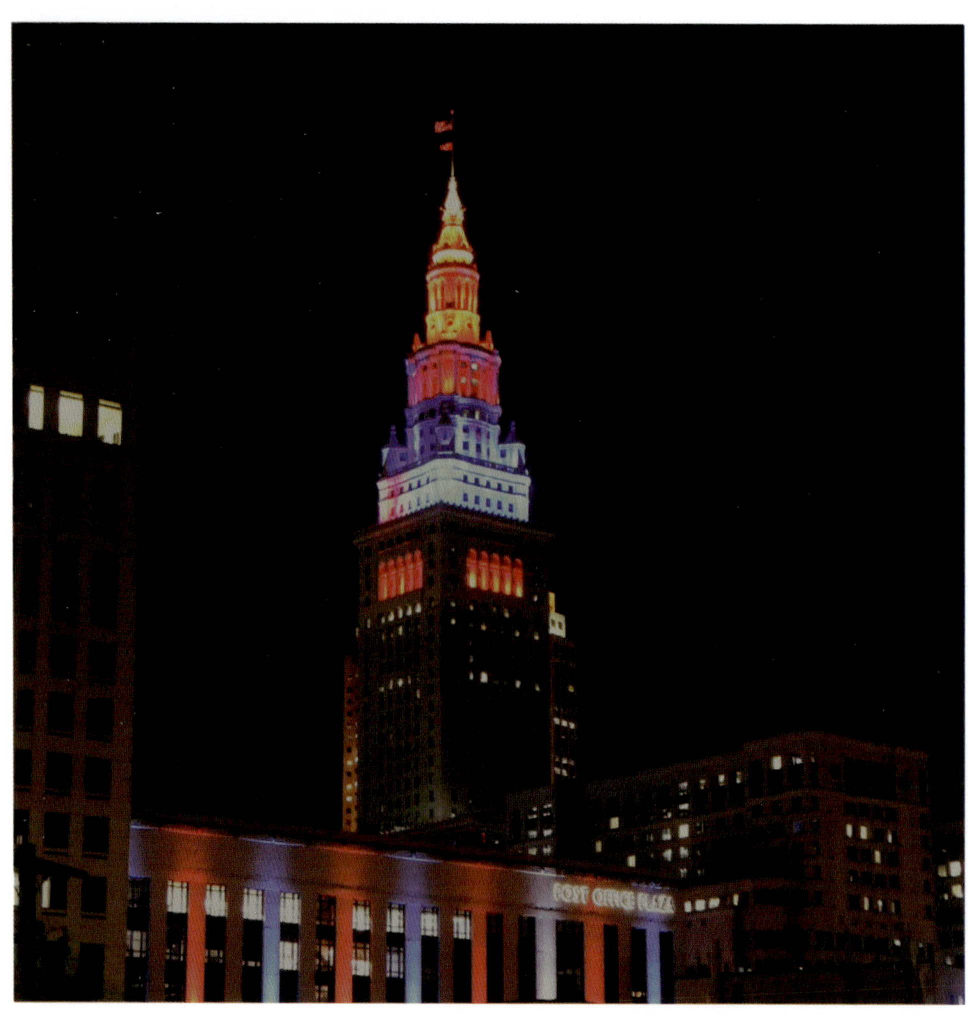

The Terminal Tower is lit up in different colors every night.

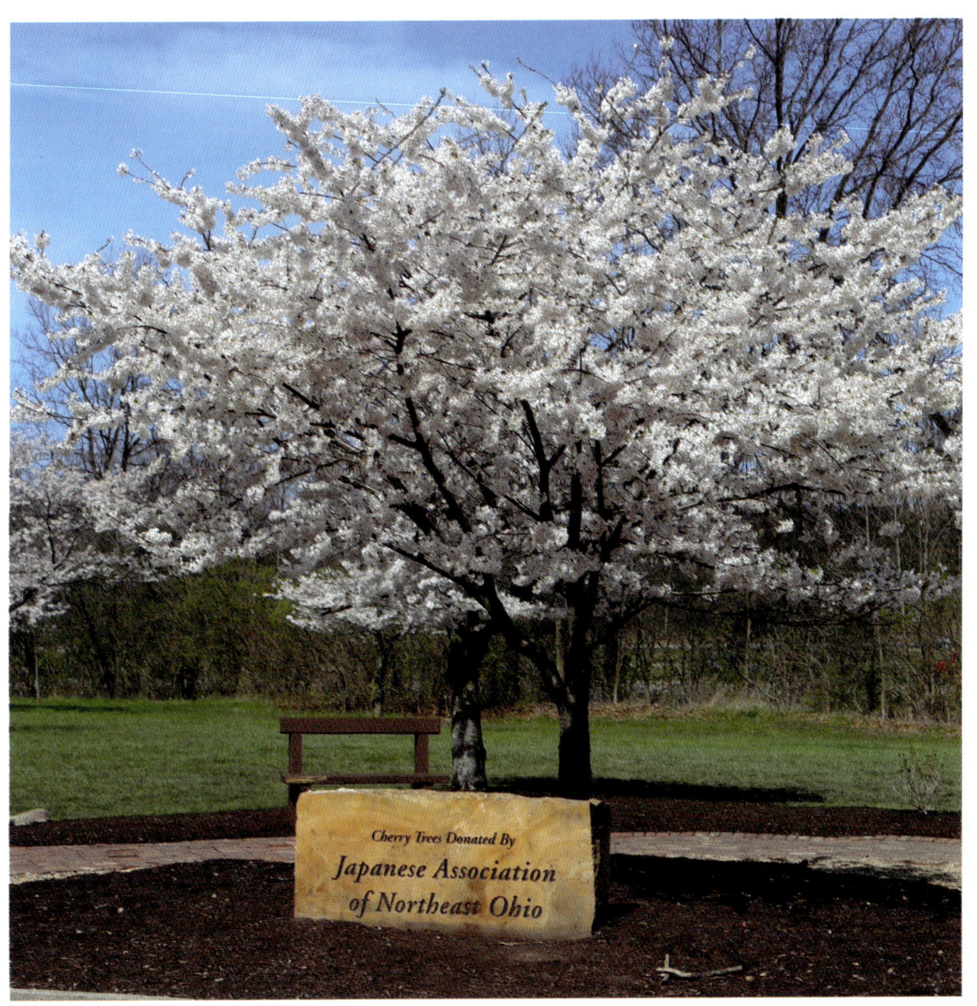

The cherry blossoms at Brookside Reservation

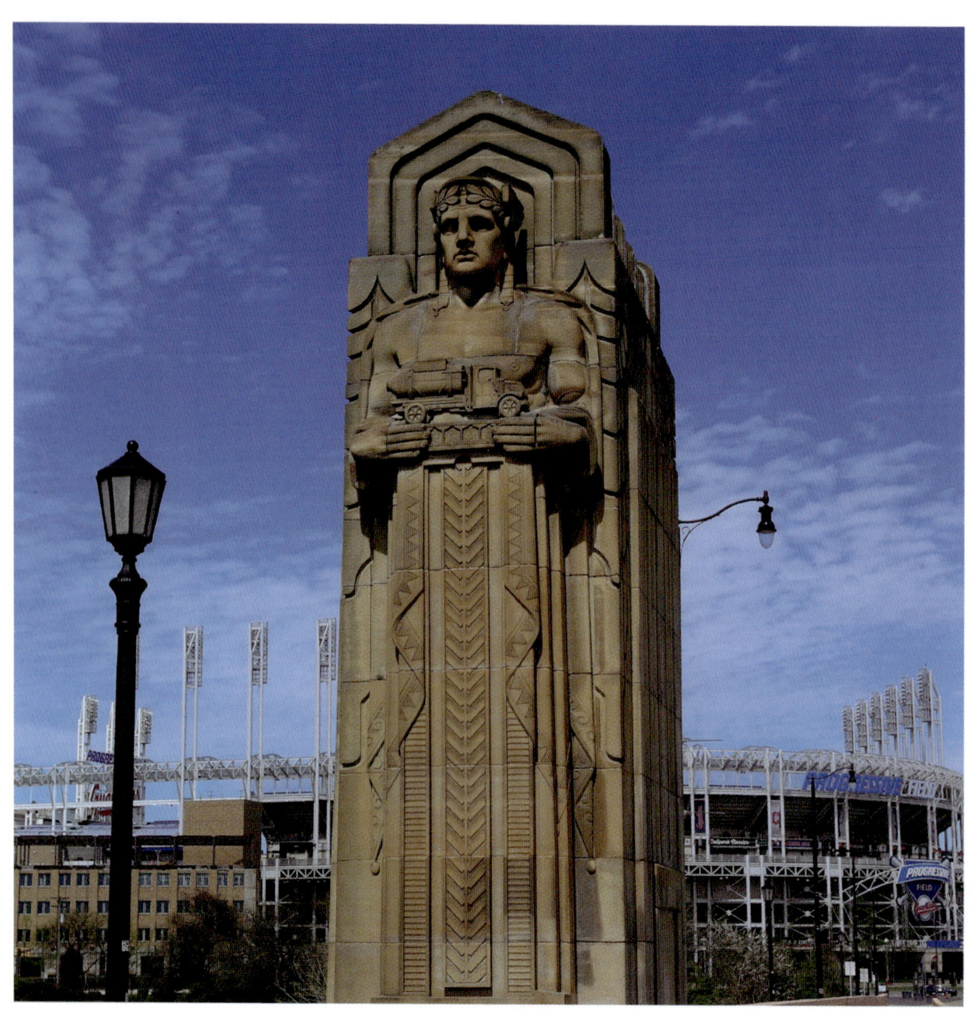

The Guardians of Transportation line the Lorain-Carnegie Bridge.

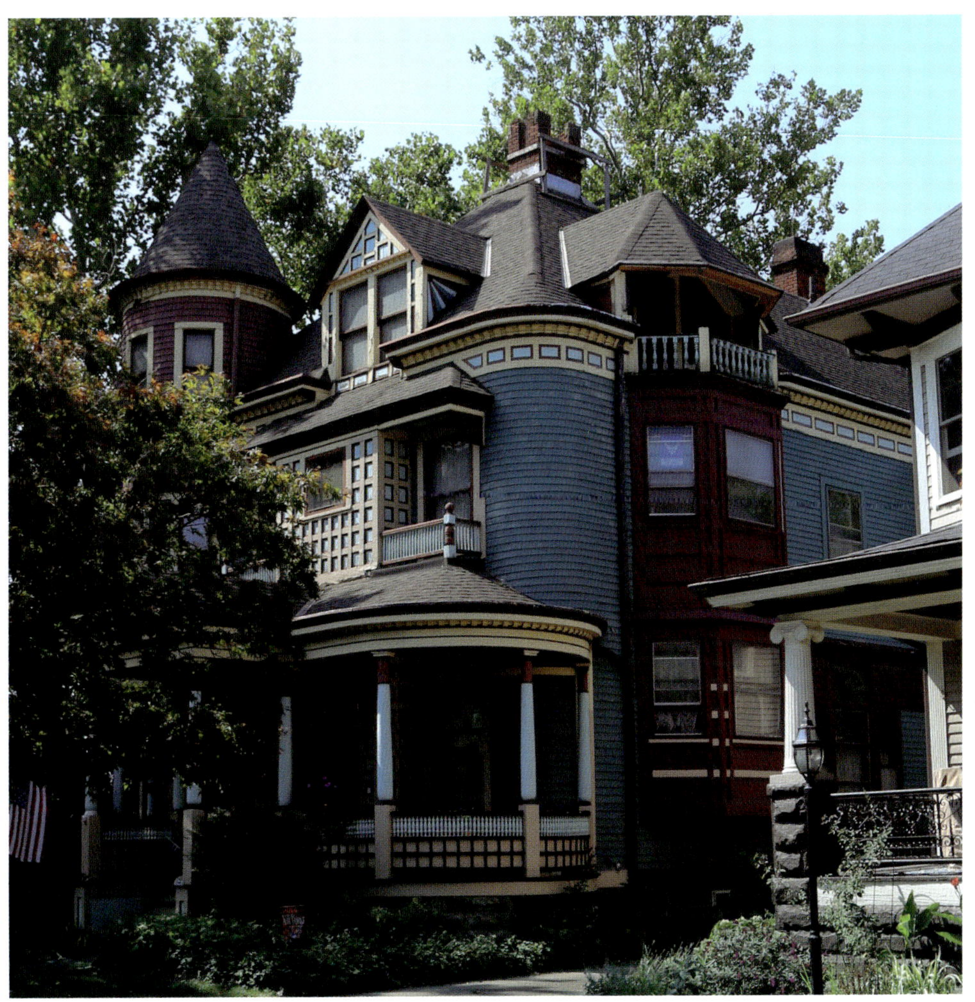

The historic Painted Lady house in Tremont

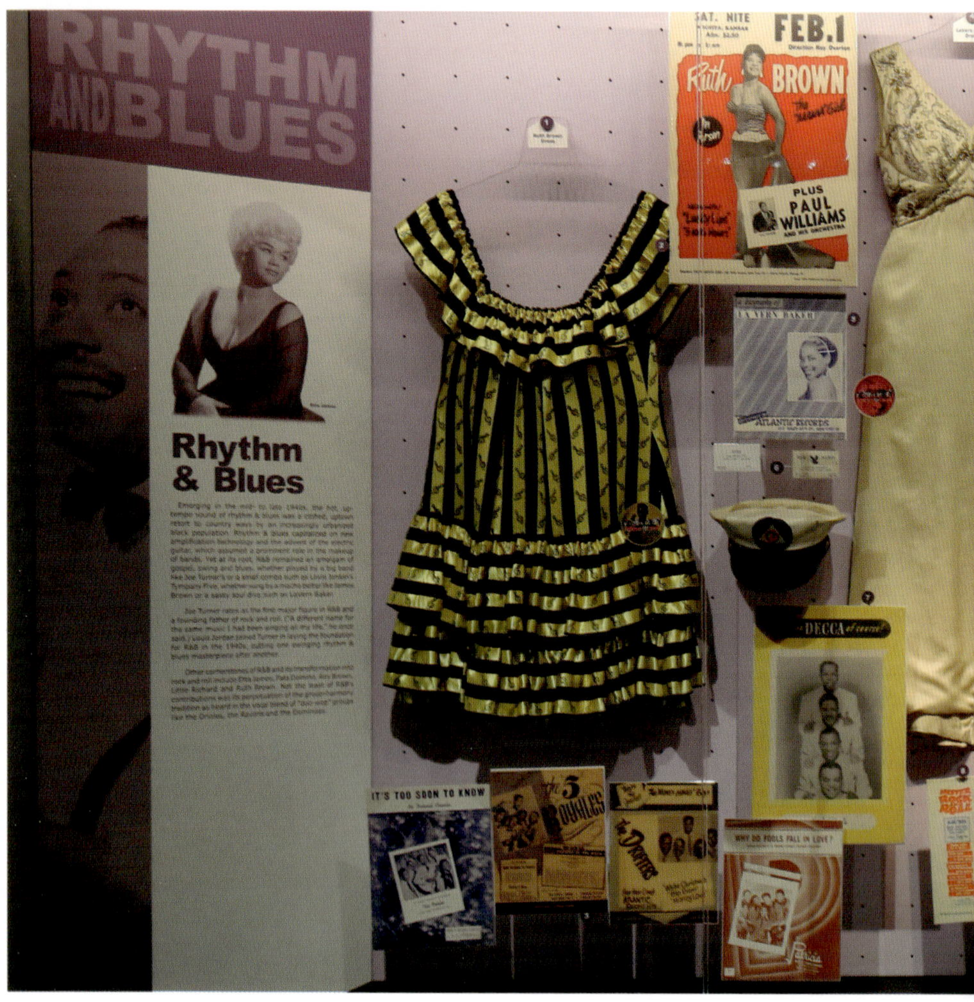
RHYTHM AND BLUES
Rhythm & Blues
SAT. NITE
FEB. 1
Ruth BROWN
PLUS
PAUL WILLIAMS
AND HIS ORCHESTRA
ATLANTIC RECORDS
DECCA
IT'S TOO SOON TO KNOW
The 5 Royales
The Drifters
WHY DO FOOLS FALL IN LOVE?

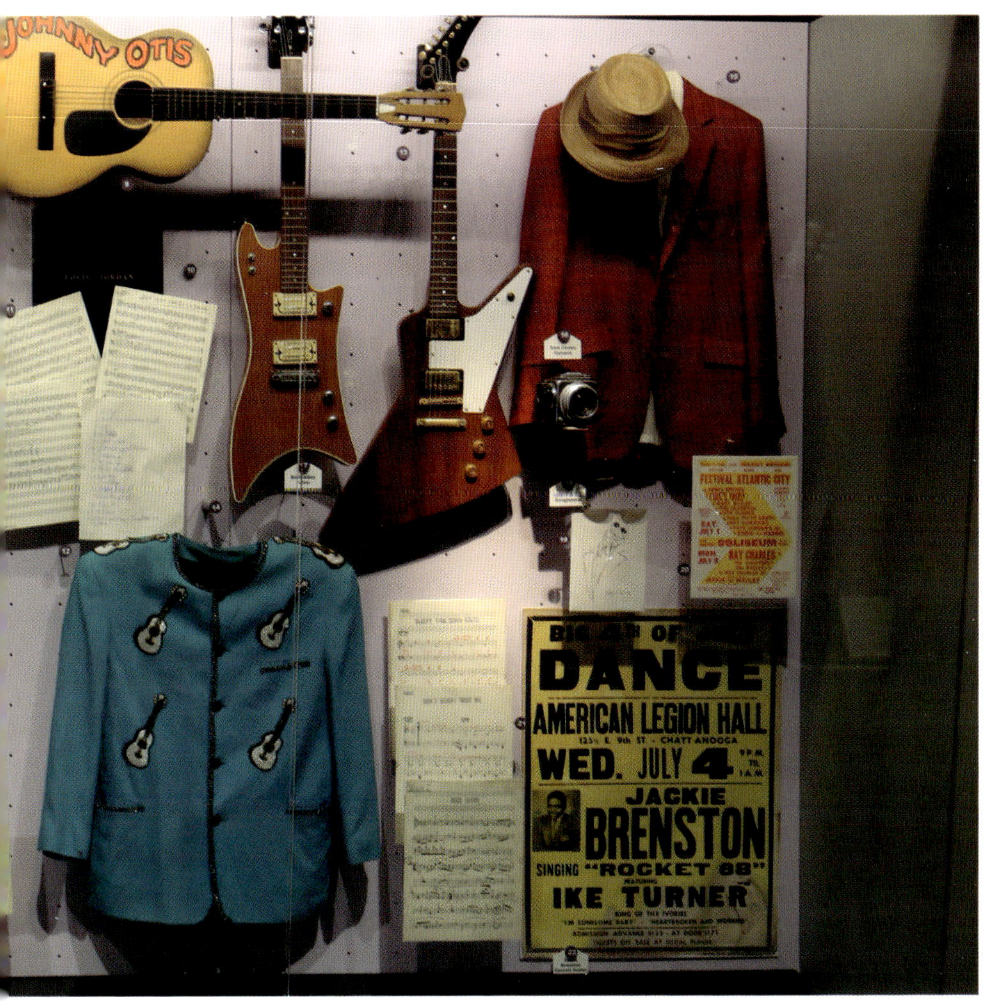

Rhythm-and-blues exhibit at the Rock & Roll Hall of Fame

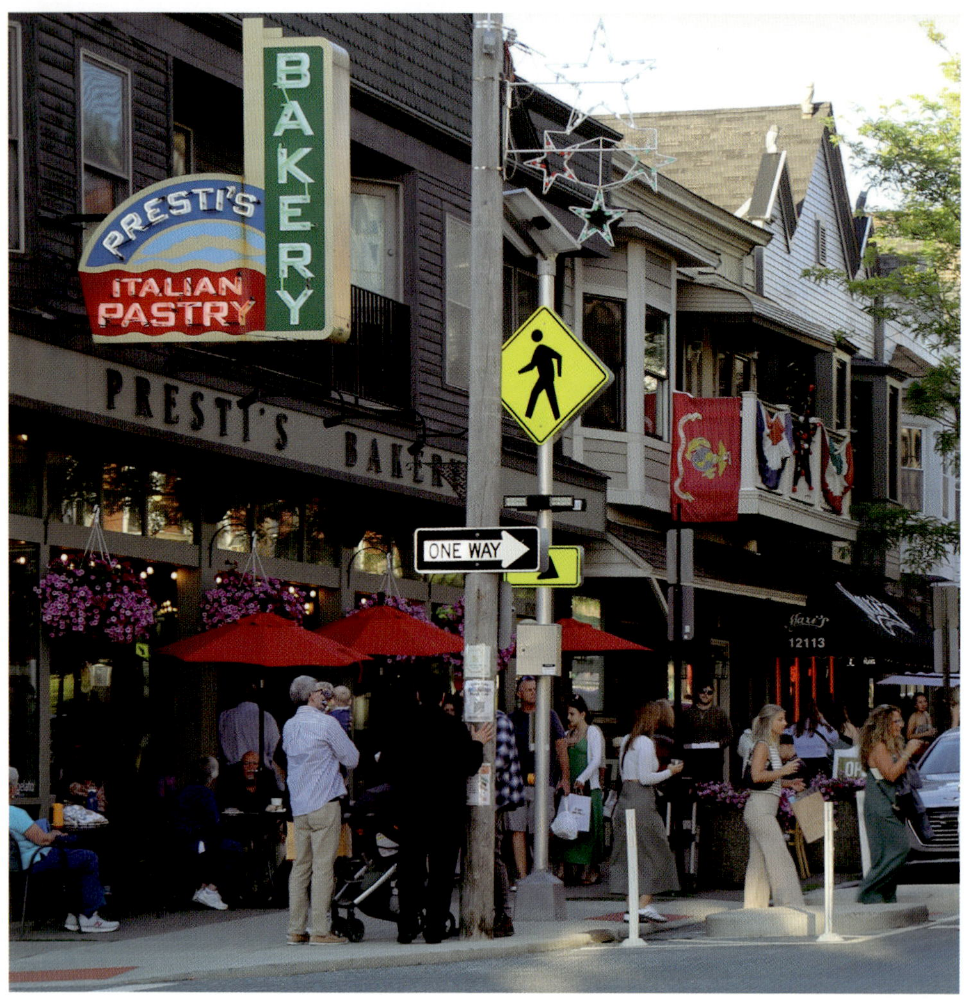

Along Mayfield Road in the historic Little Italy neighborhood

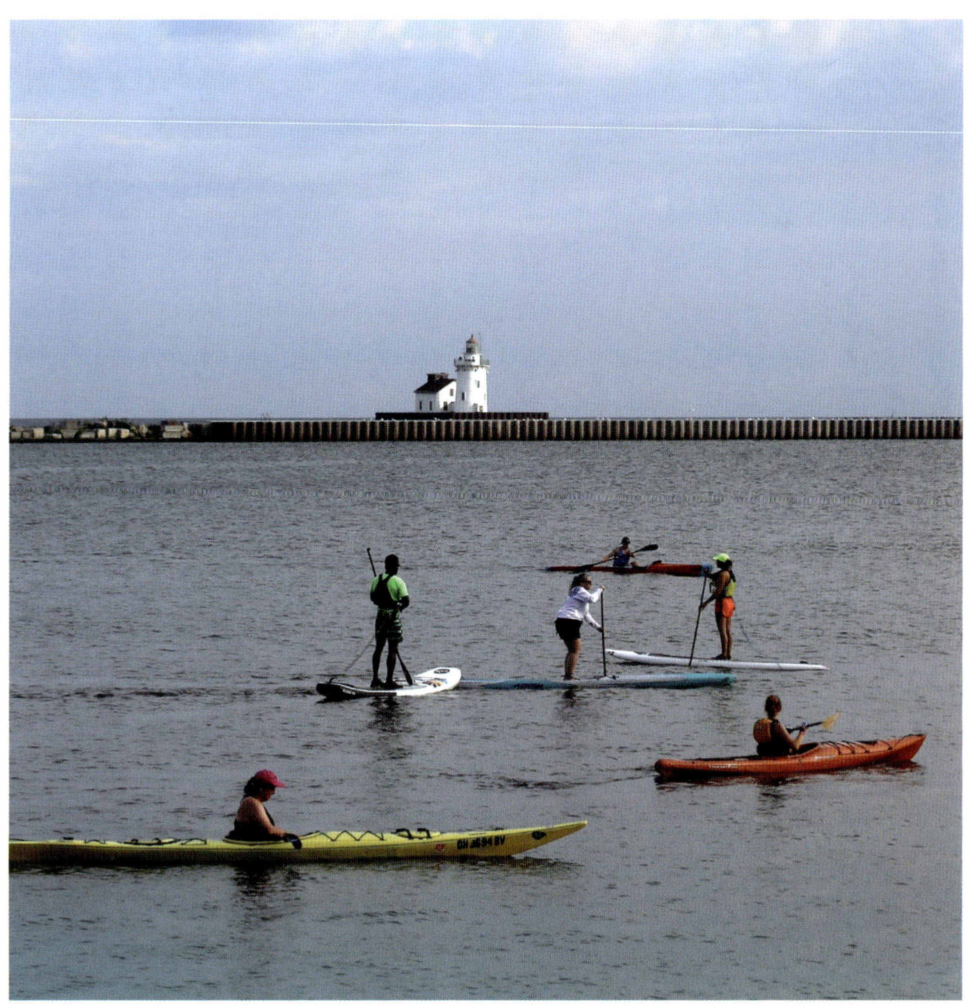

Watercraft in front of the Cleveland Harbor West Pierhead Lighthouse

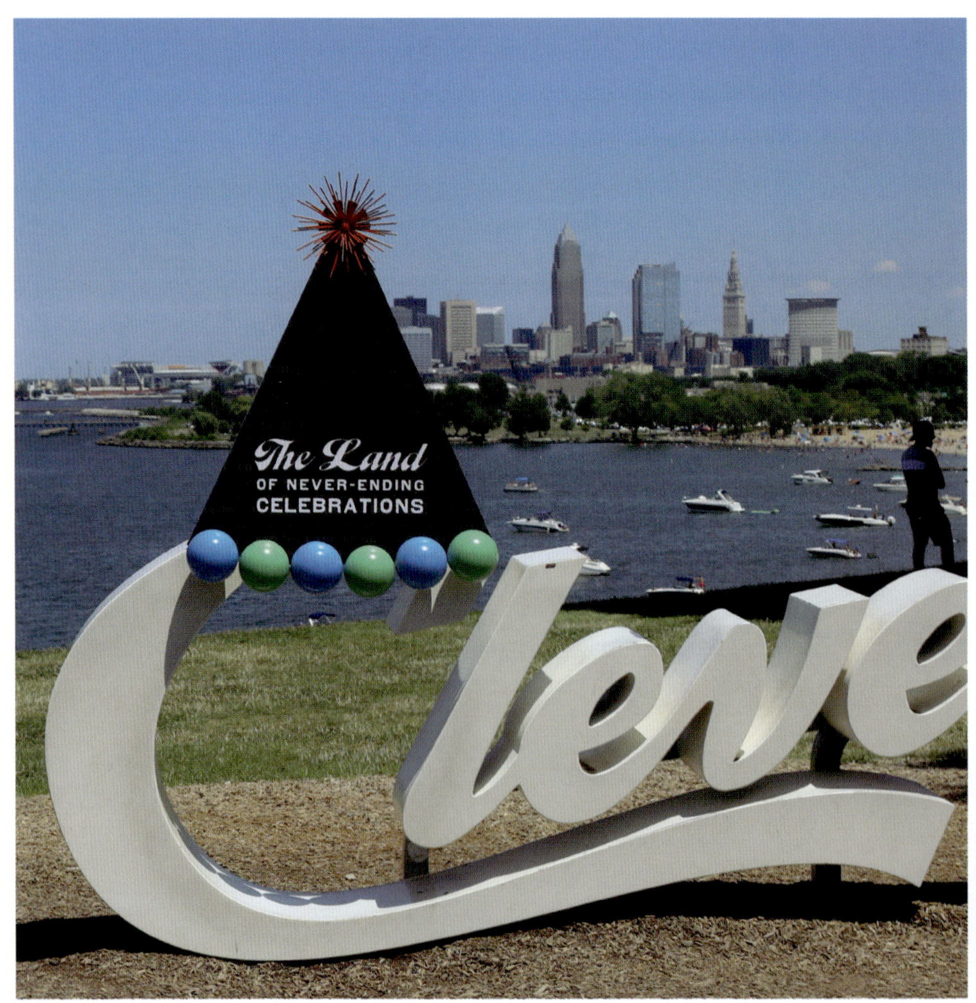

The Cleveland Script Sign at Edgewater Park

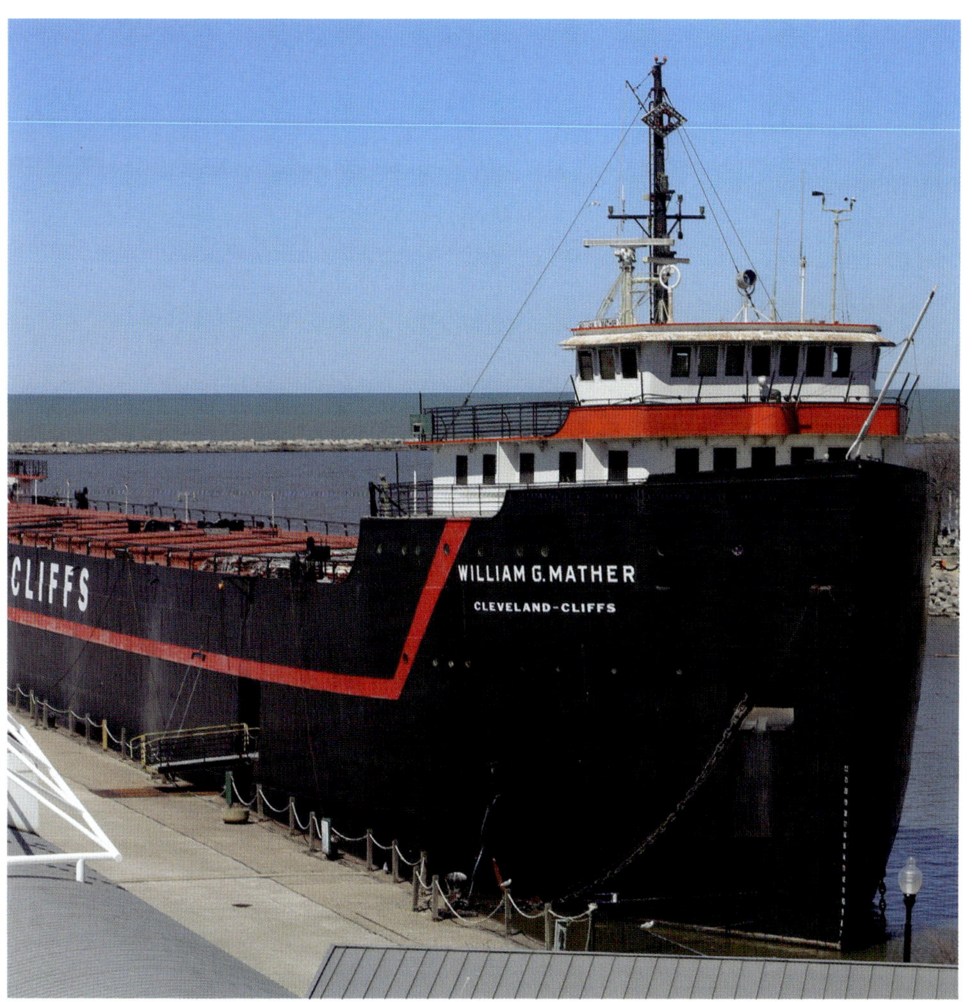

The steamship *William G. Mather* is now a restored museum ship.

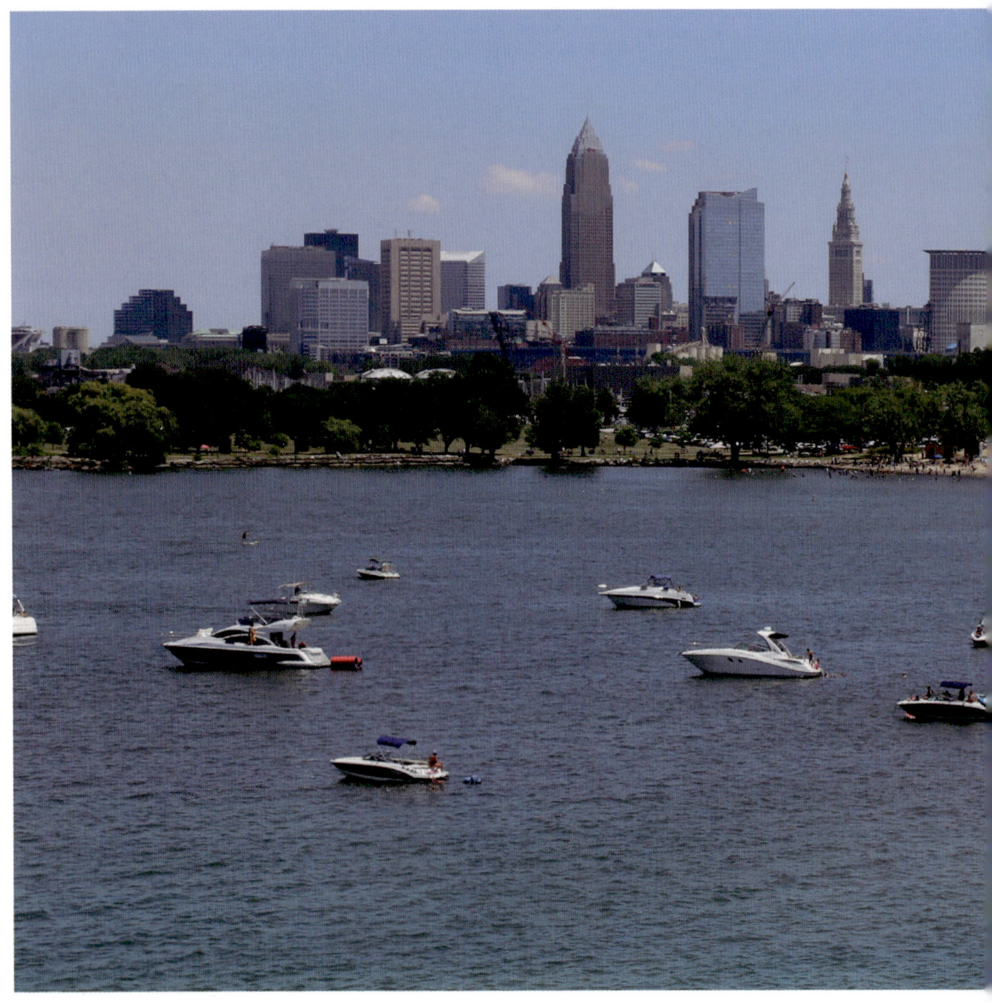

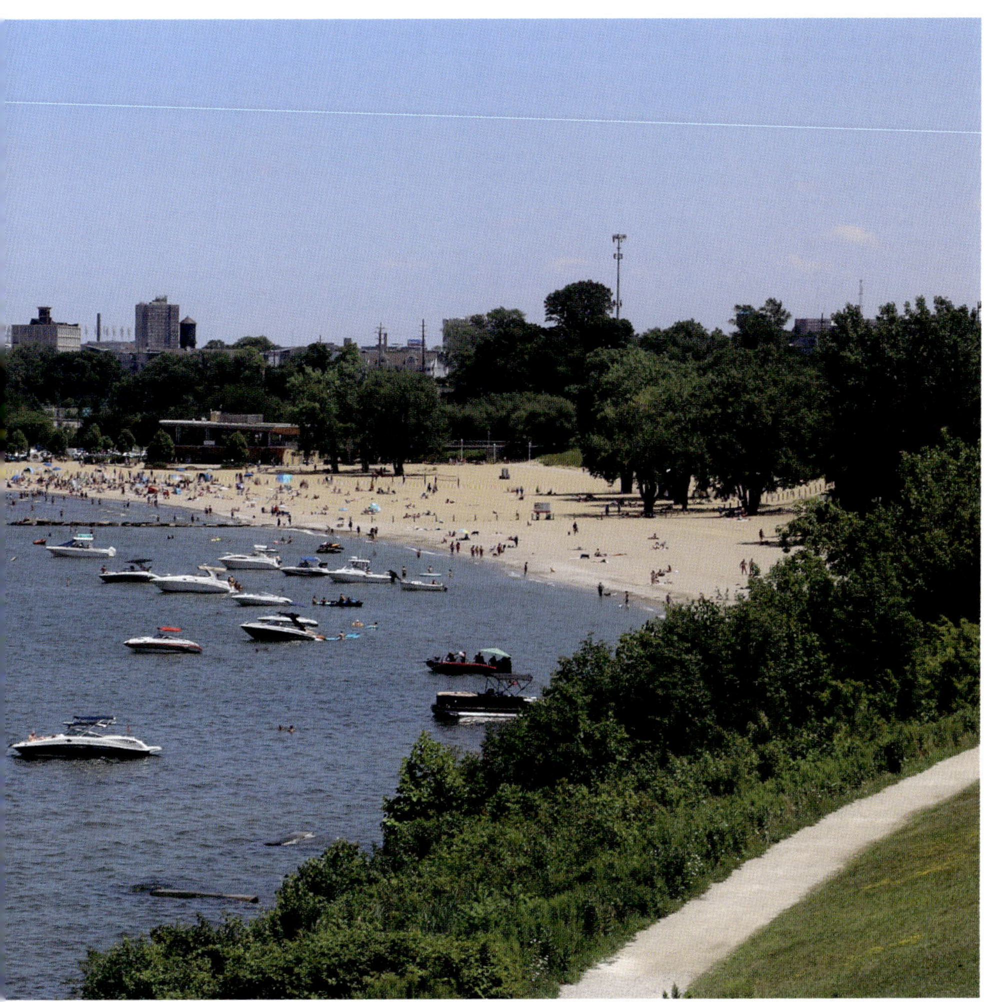

Boats frequently surround Edgewater Beach.

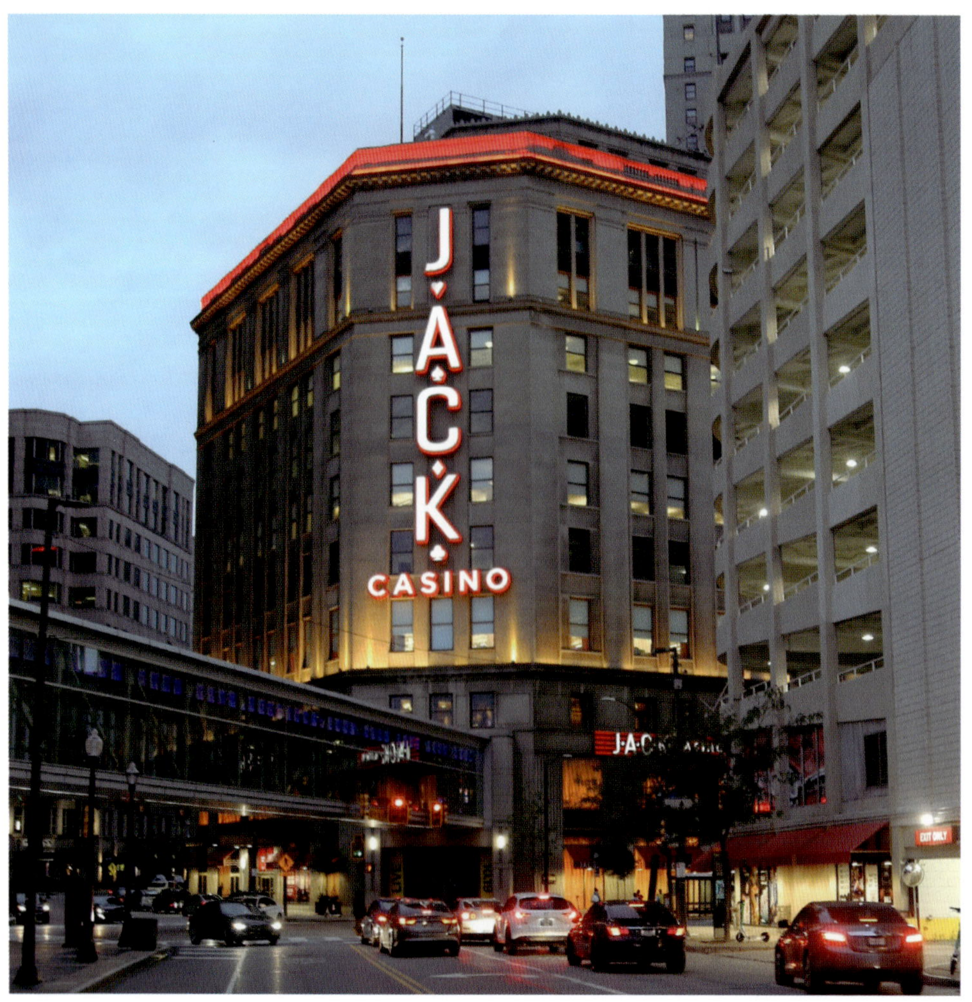

JACK Cleveland Casino

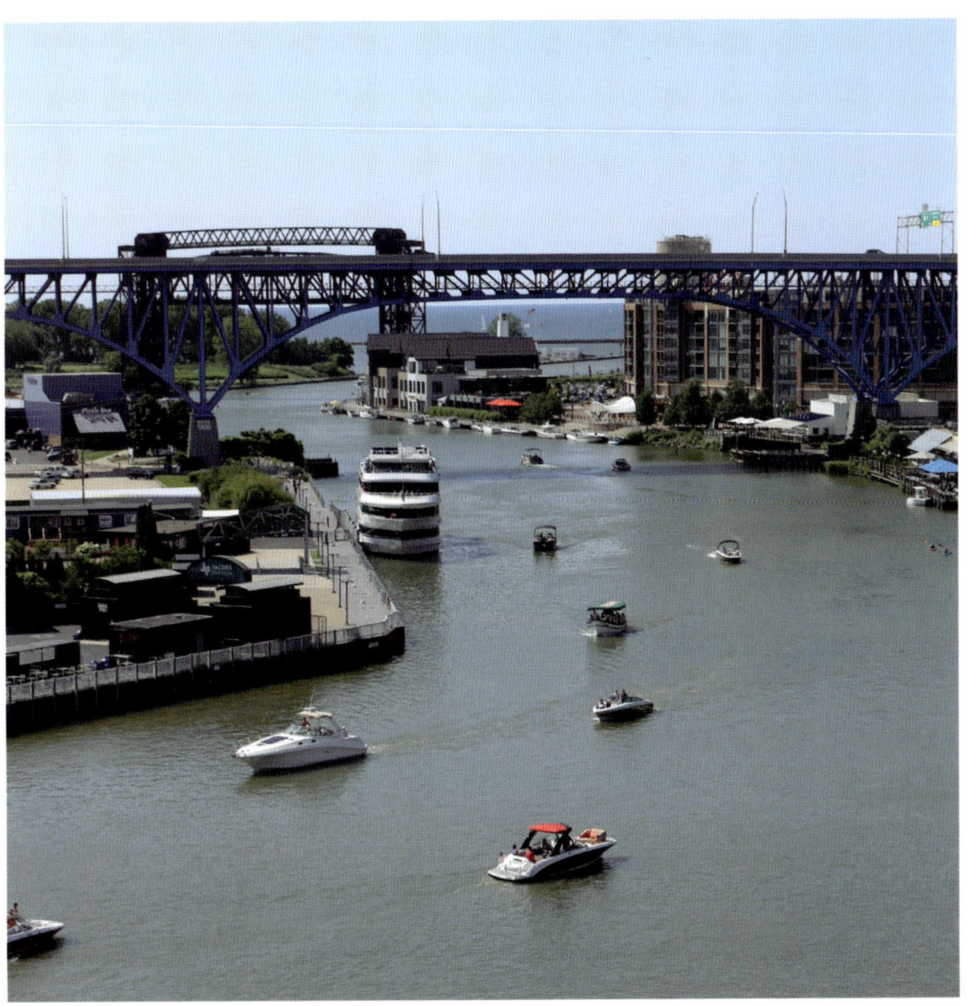

Boaters traveling down the Cuyahoga River

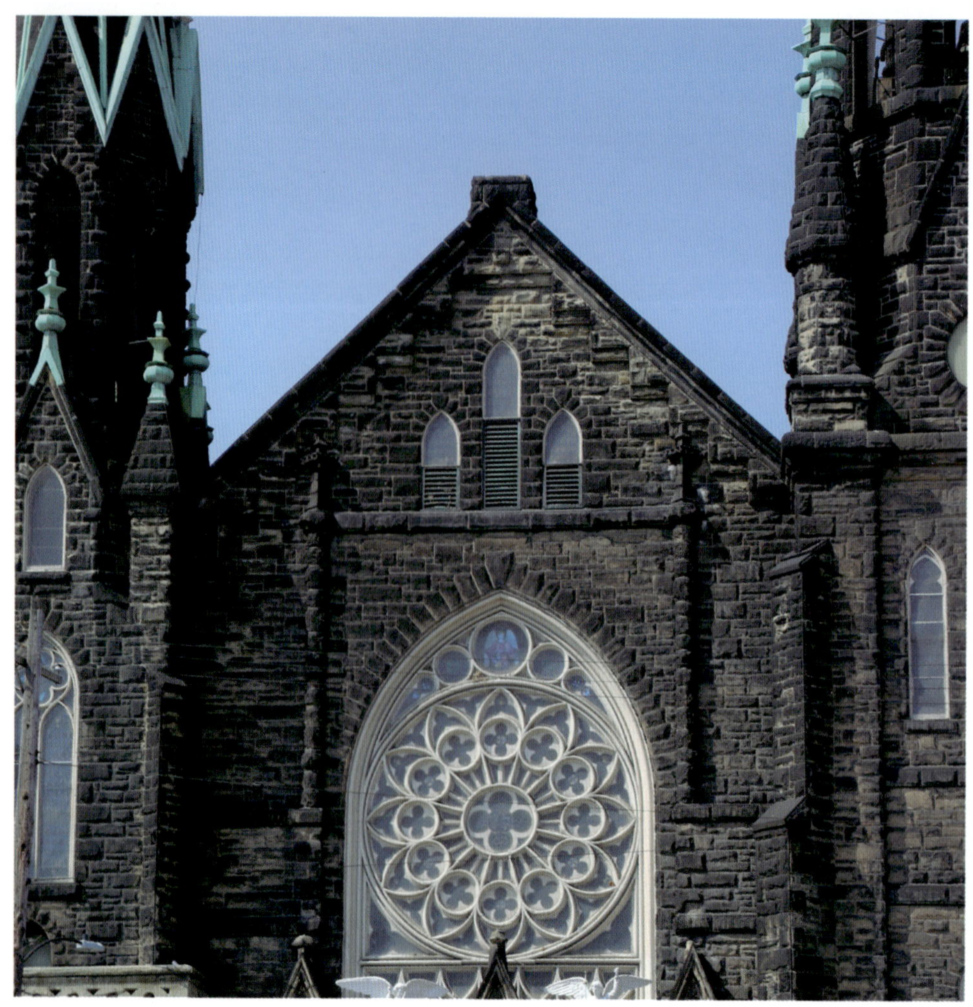

Saint Michael the Archangel Roman Catholic Church

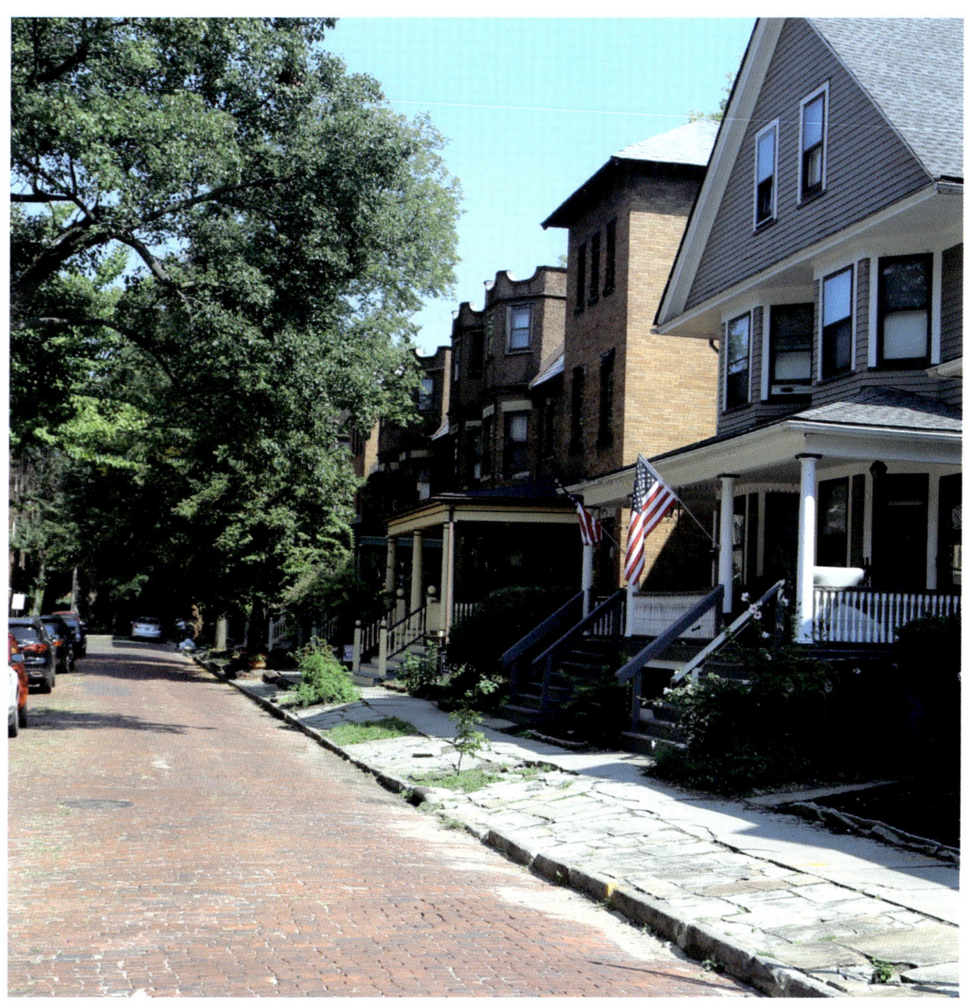

Hessler Road is designated as a historic district.

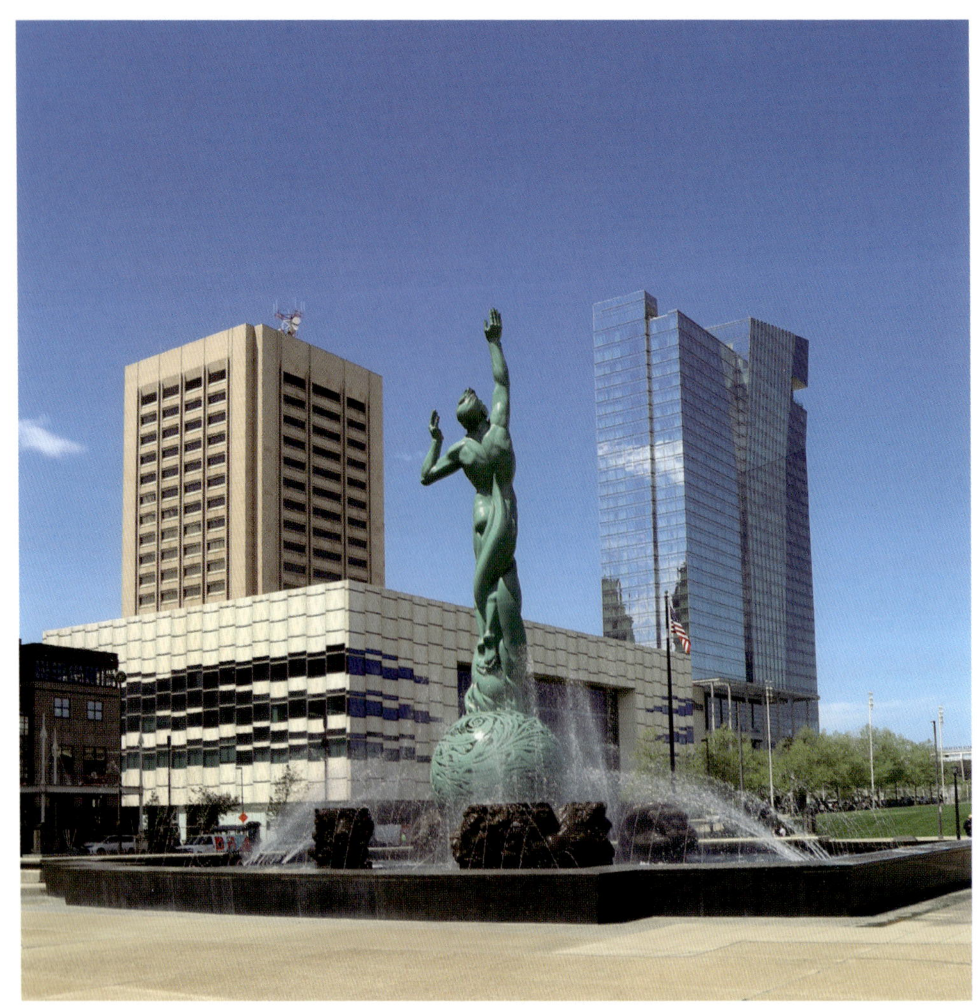

The Fountain of Eternal Life in downtown Cleveland

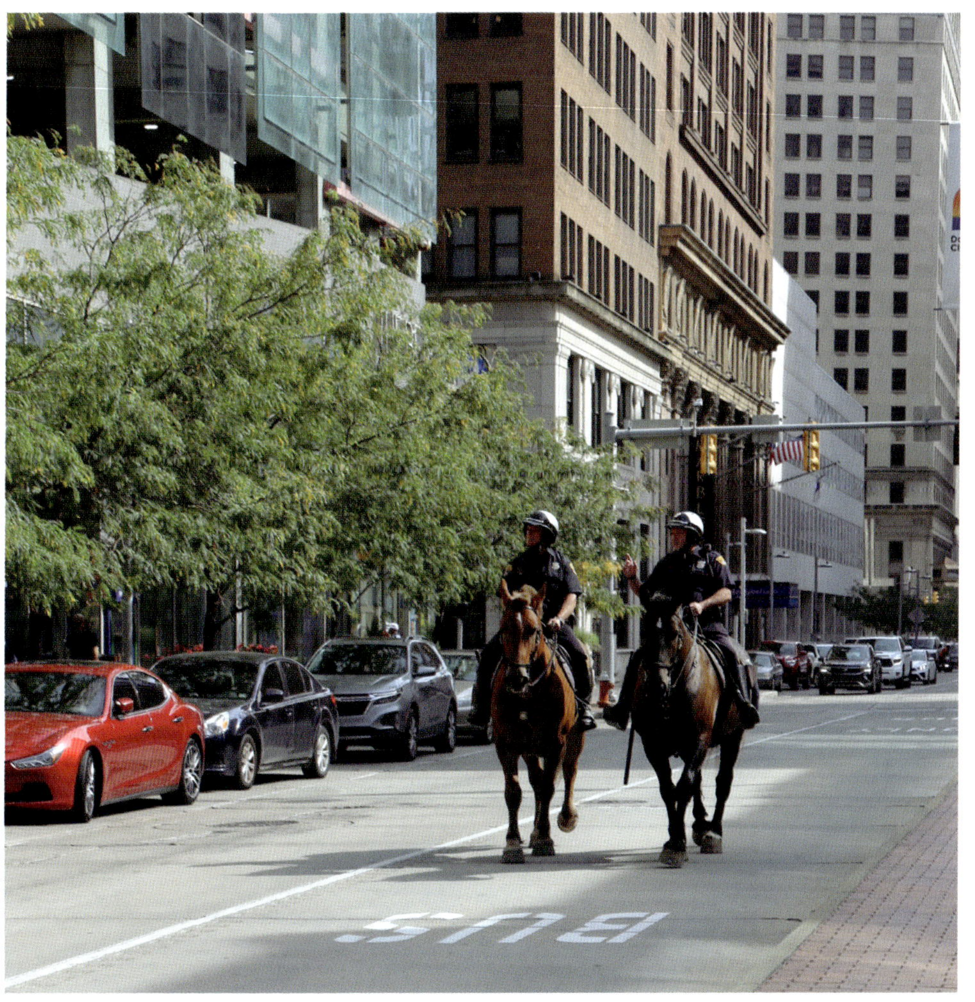

Cleveland's finest patrolling Euclid Avenue

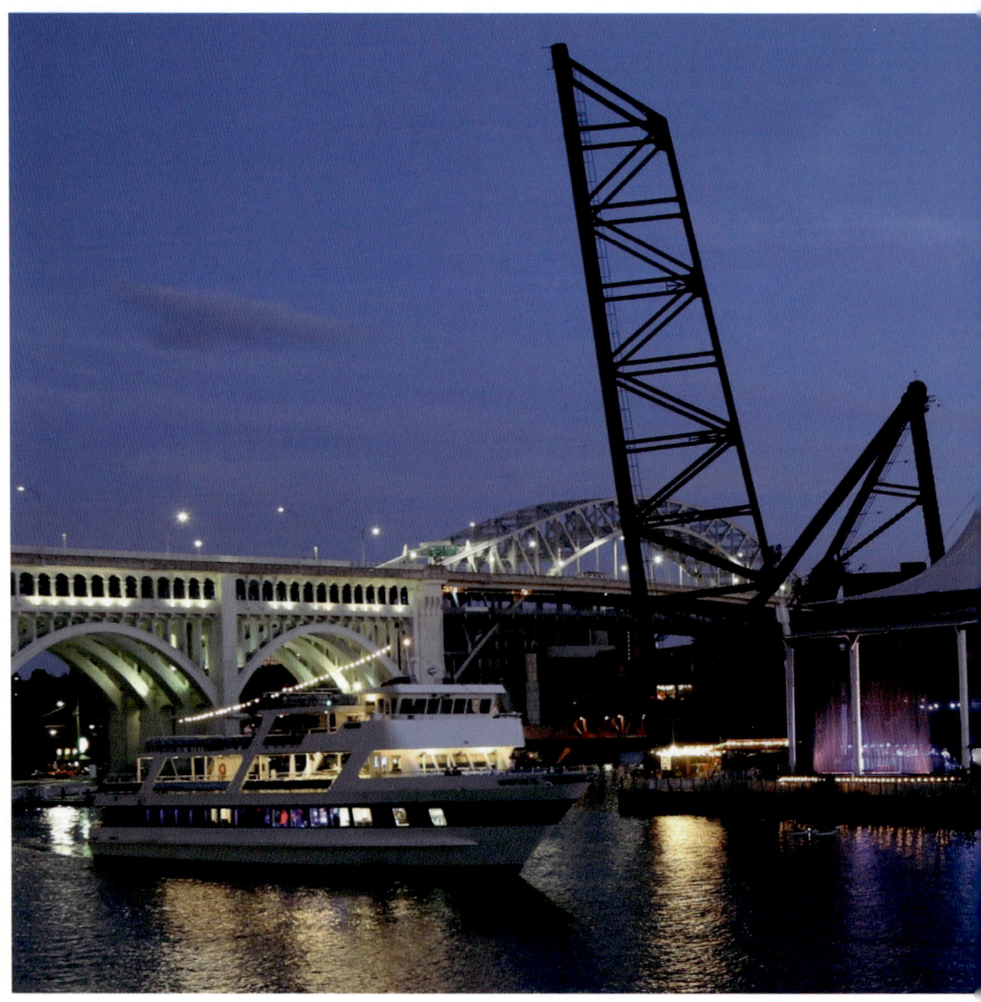

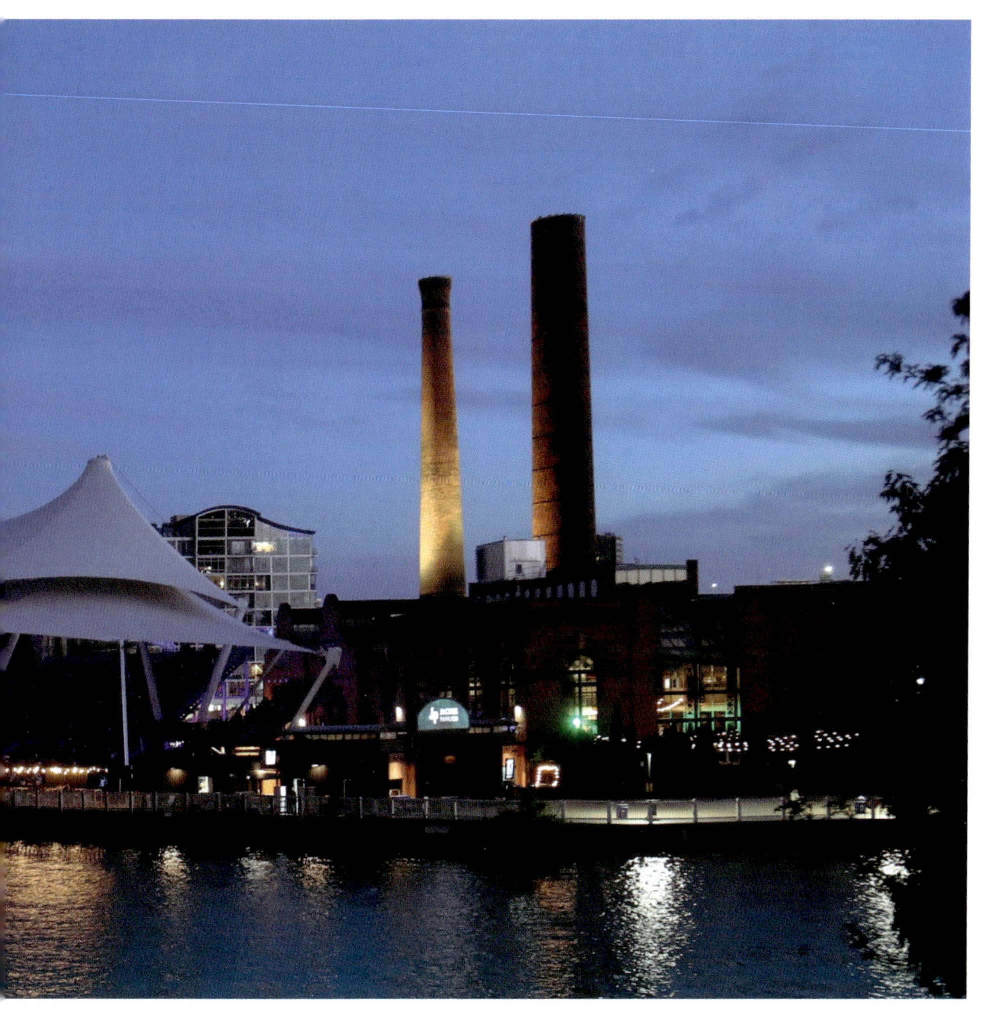

A concert begins at Jacob's Pavilion.

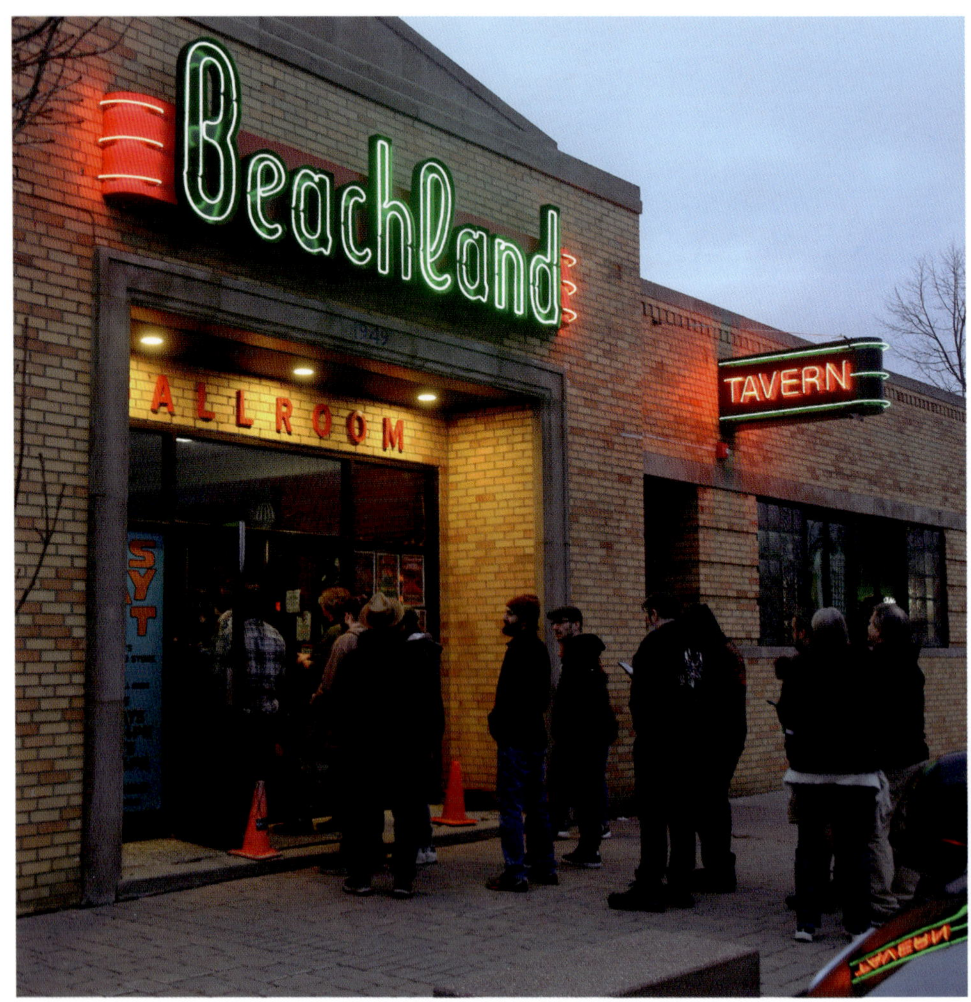

 The Beachland Ballroom & Tavern in the Waterloo Arts District

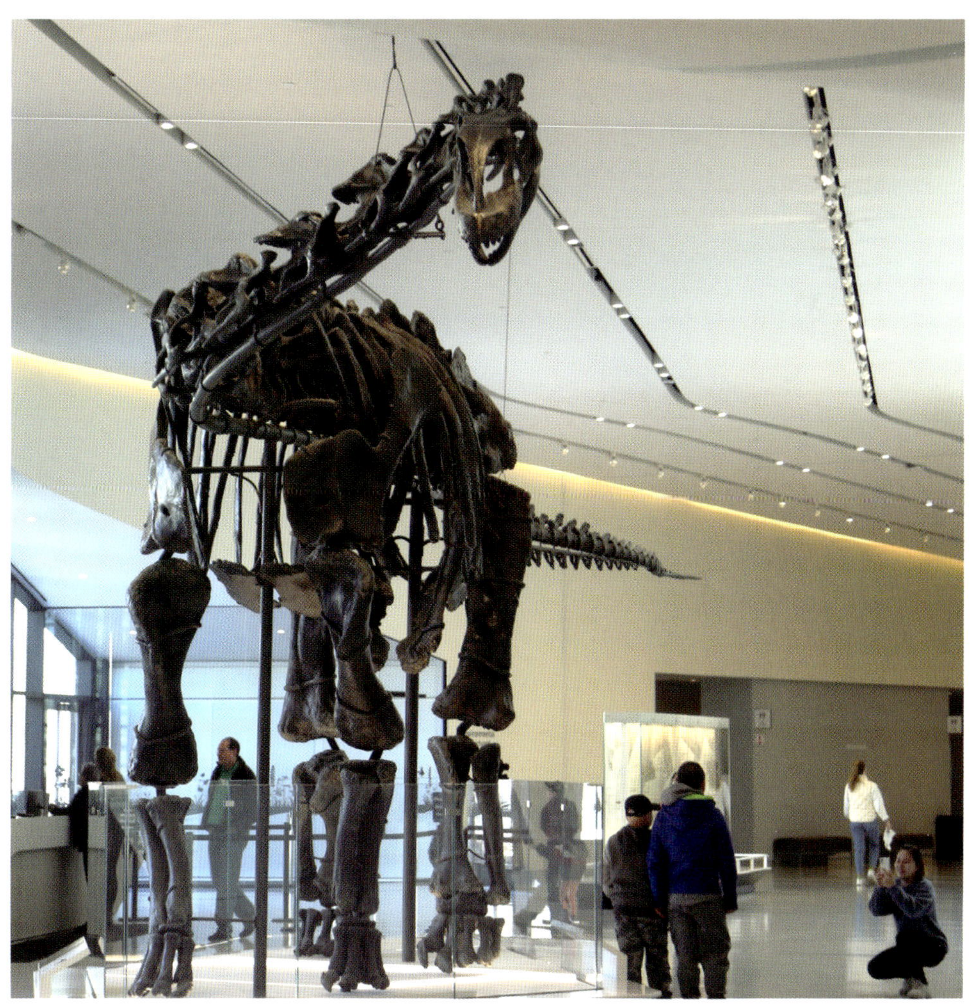

The dinosaur known as "Happy" at the Cleveland Museum of Natural History

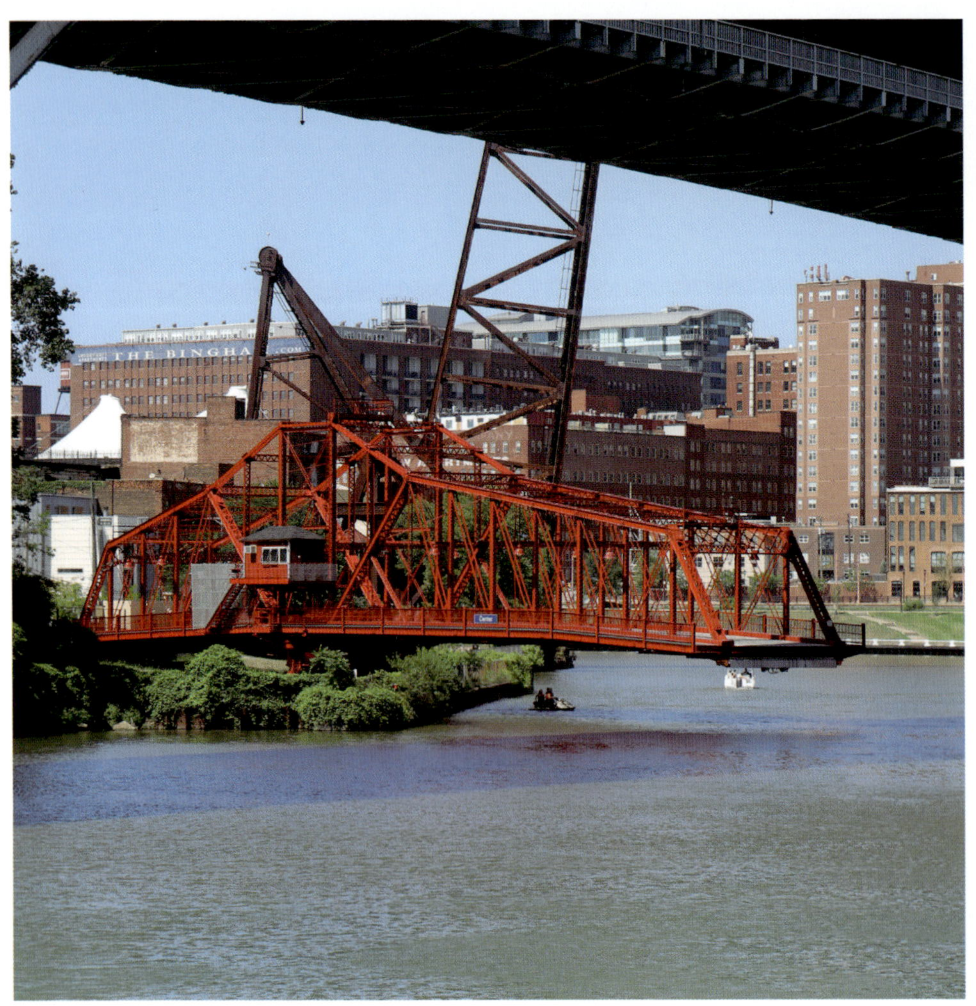

The Center Street Swing Bridge was built in 1901.

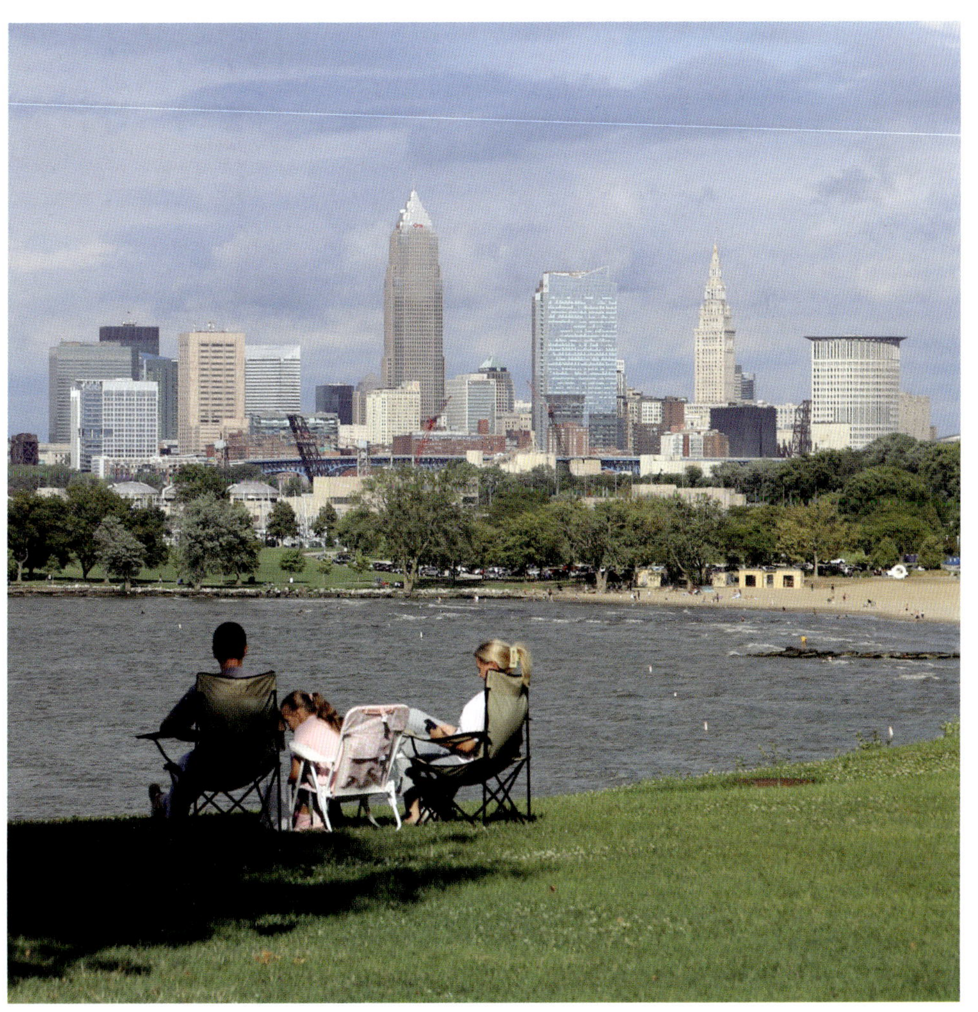

A view of downtown Cleveland from Edgewater Park

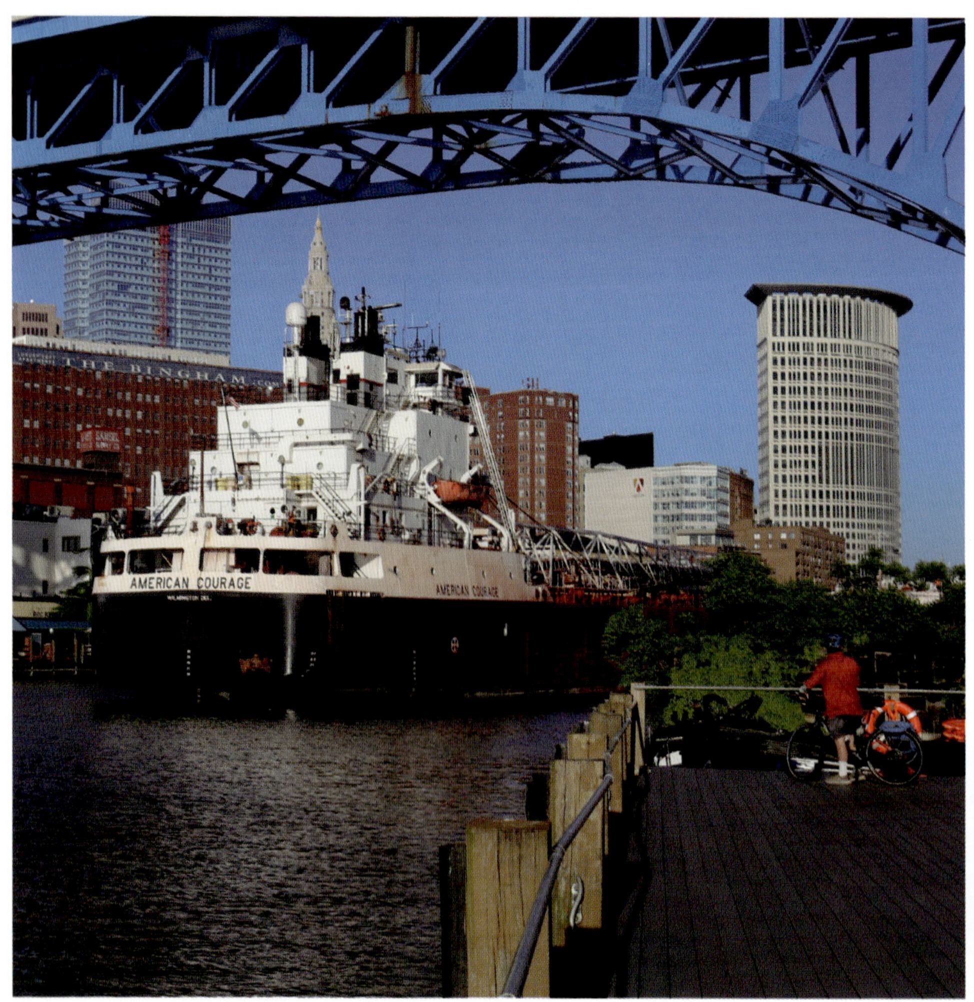

MV *American Courage* makes her way up the Cuyahoga River.

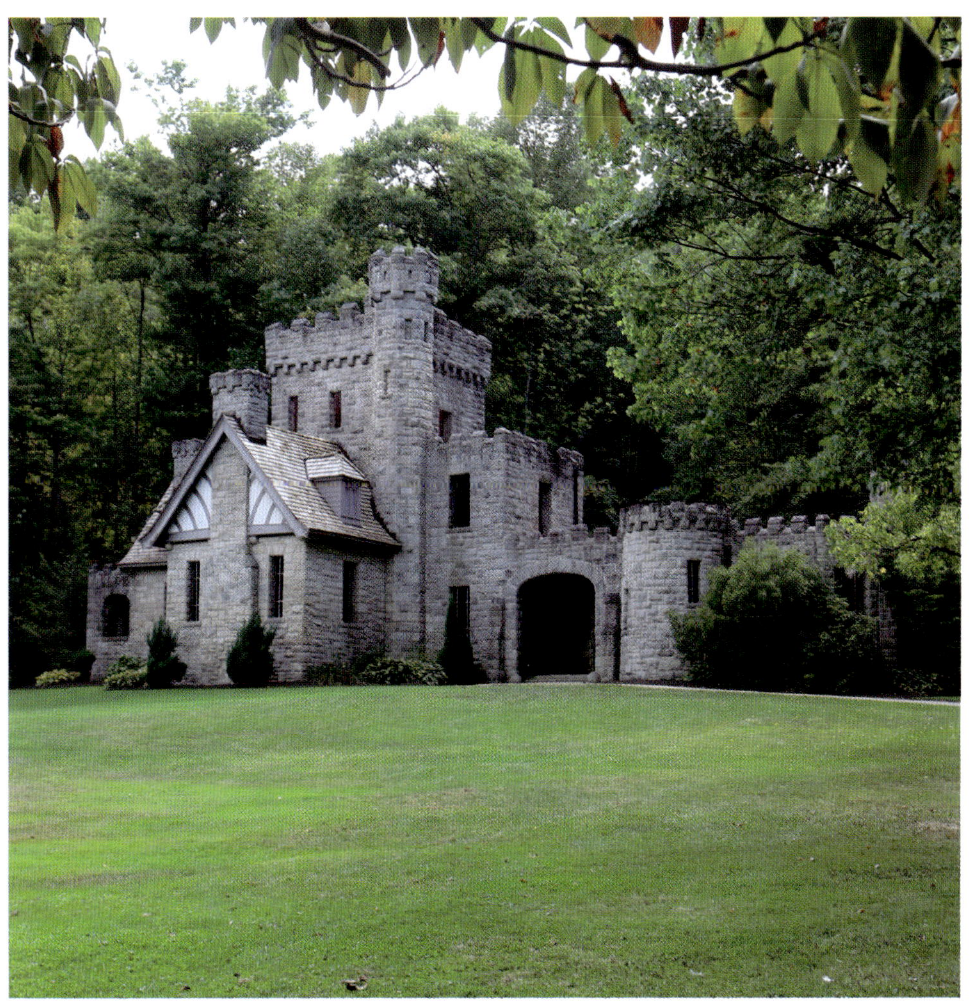

Squire's Castle in the North Chagrin Reservation

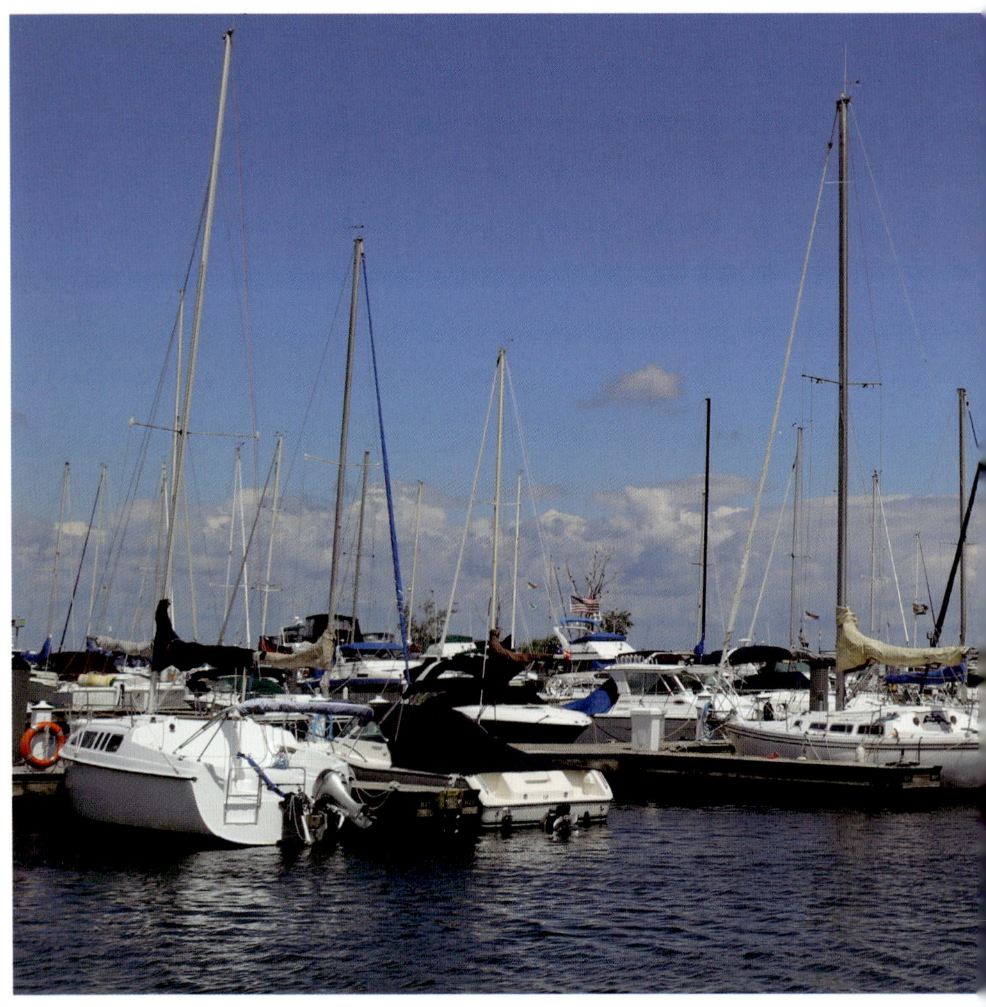

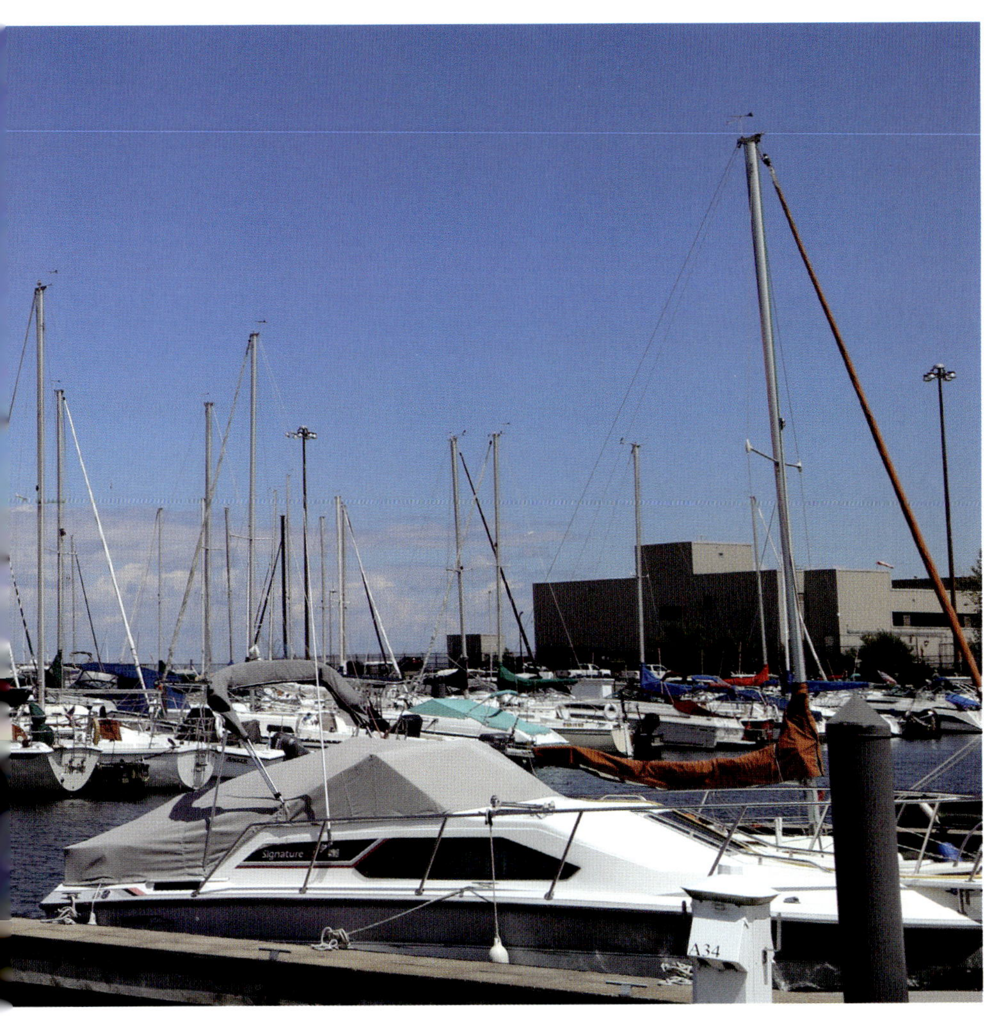

Sailboats moored at Edgewater Yacht Club

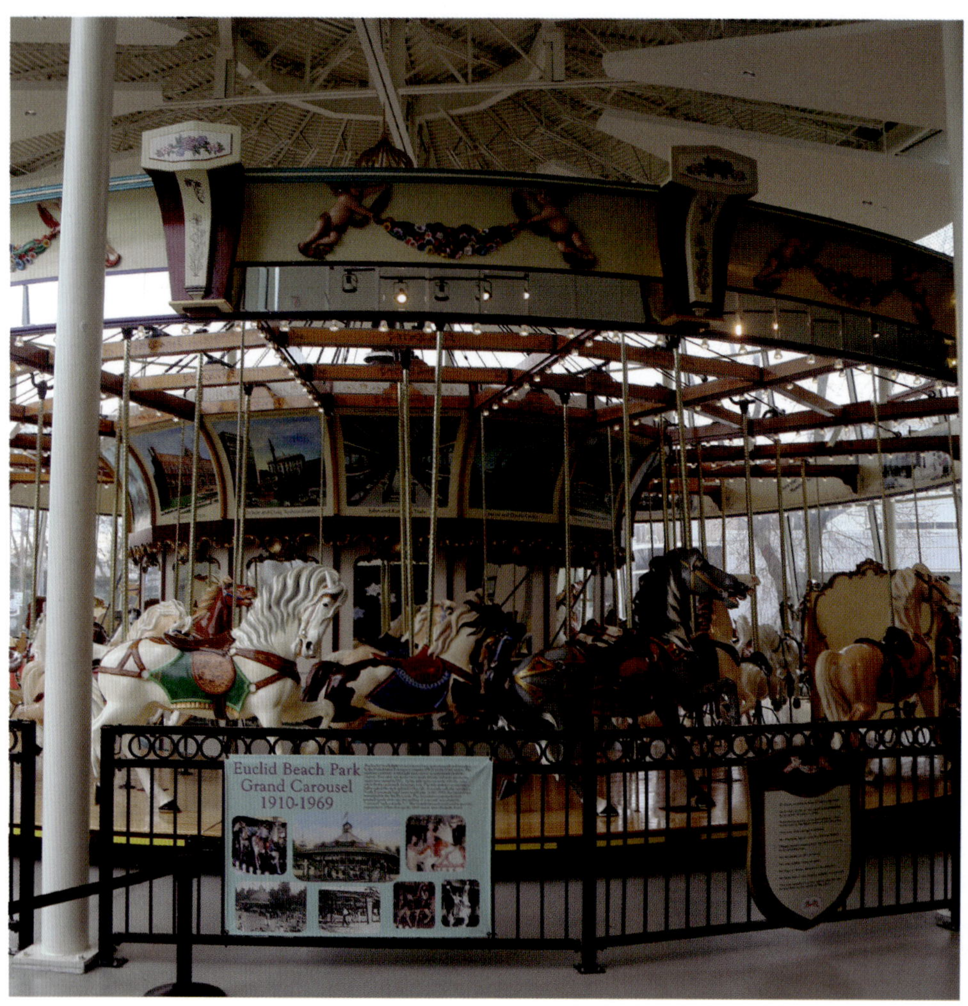

The historic Euclid Beach Grand Carousel

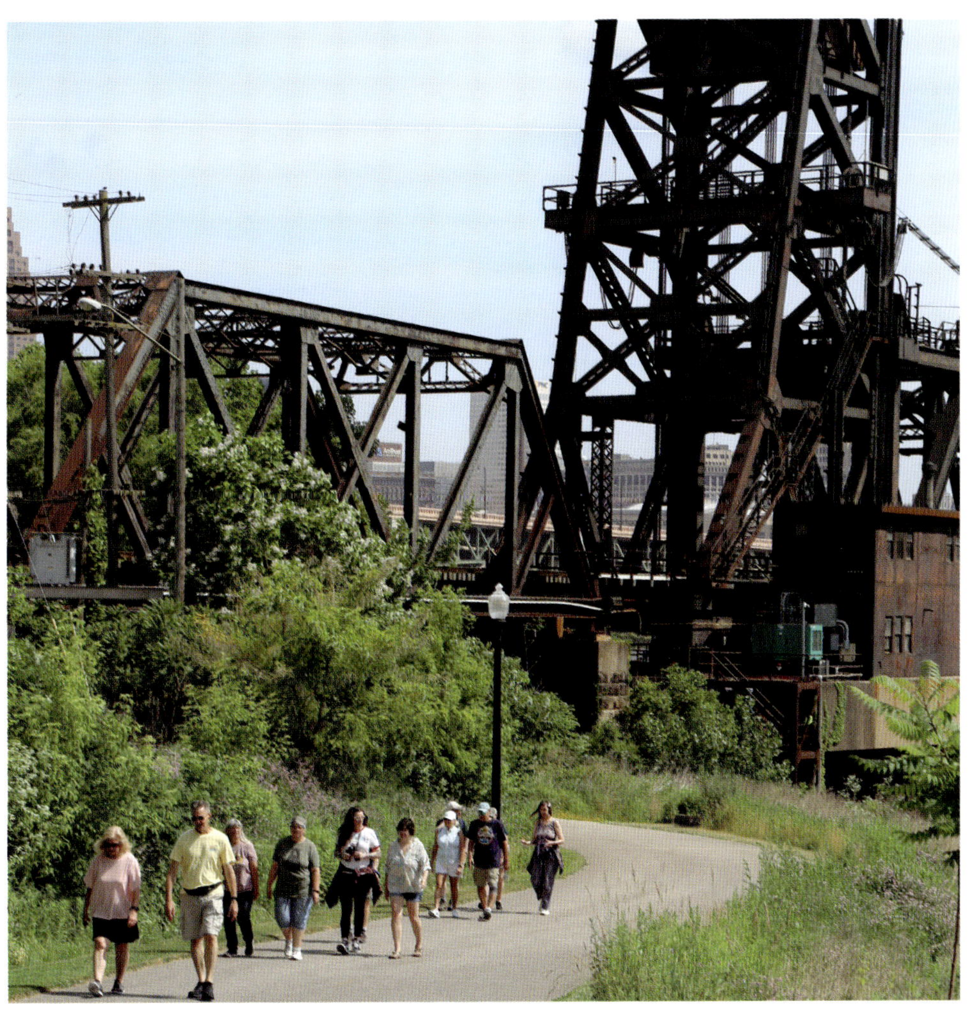

Hikers along the Ohio & Erie Canal Towpath Trail

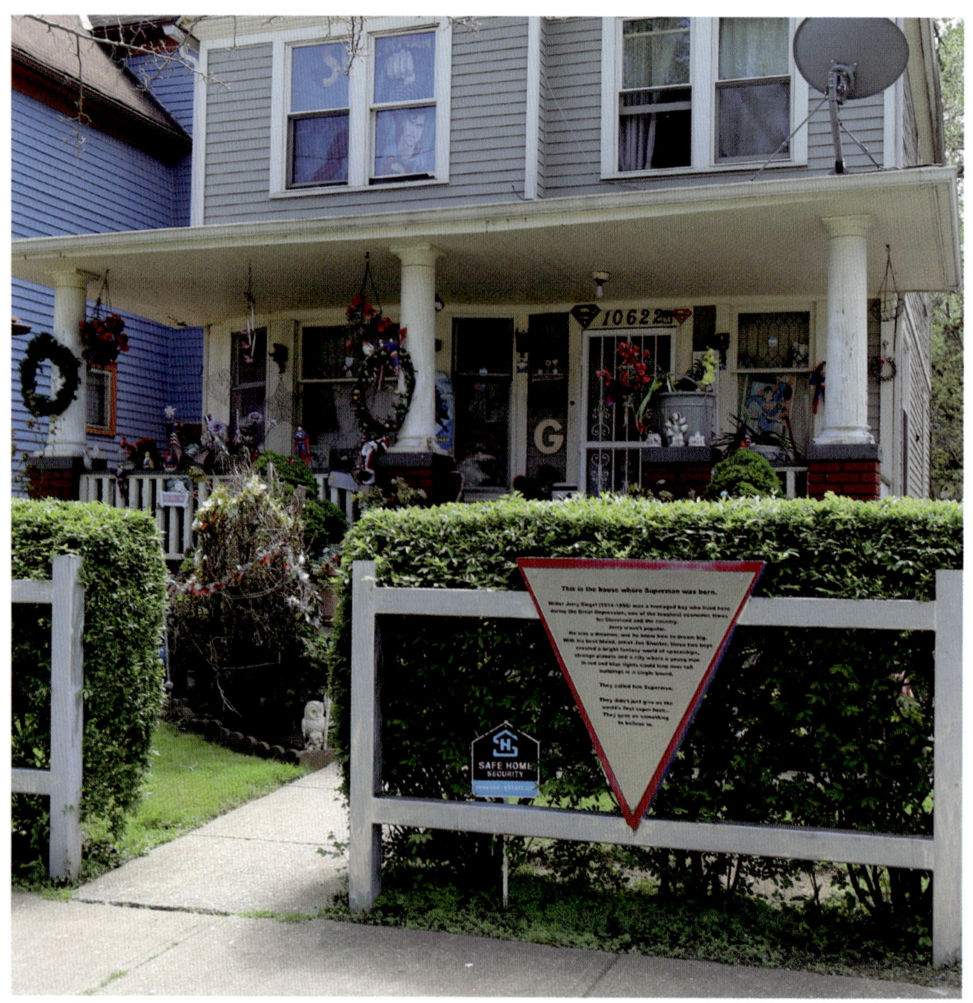

The birthplace of Superman on Kimberly Avenue in Glenville

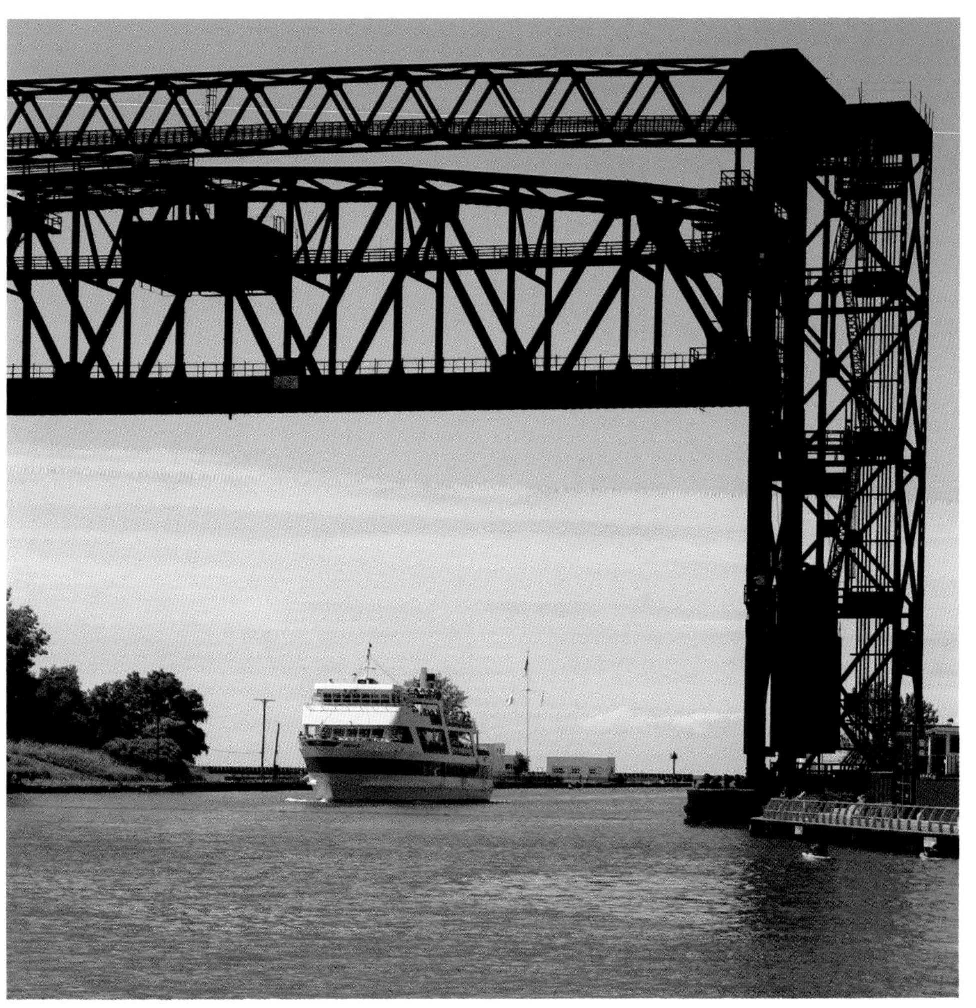

The *Goodtime III* crosses under the Iron Curtain Bridge.

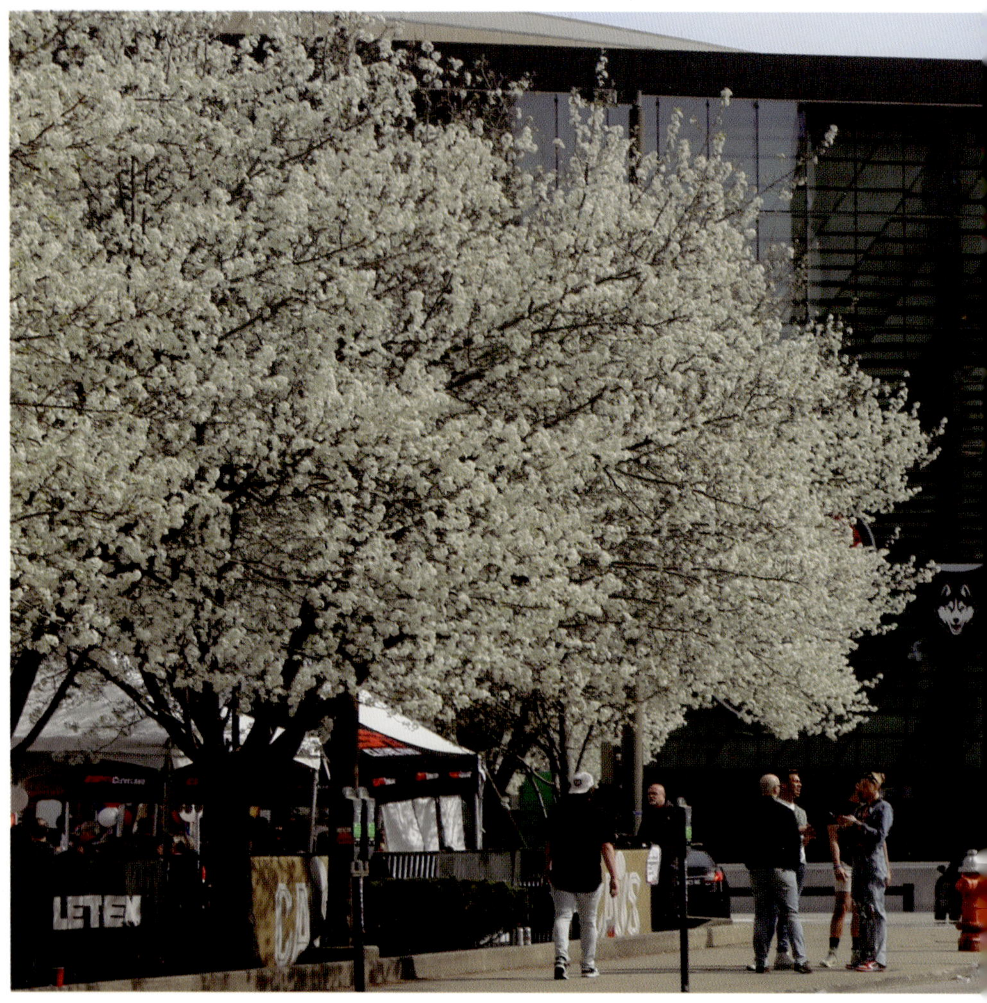
LETEN

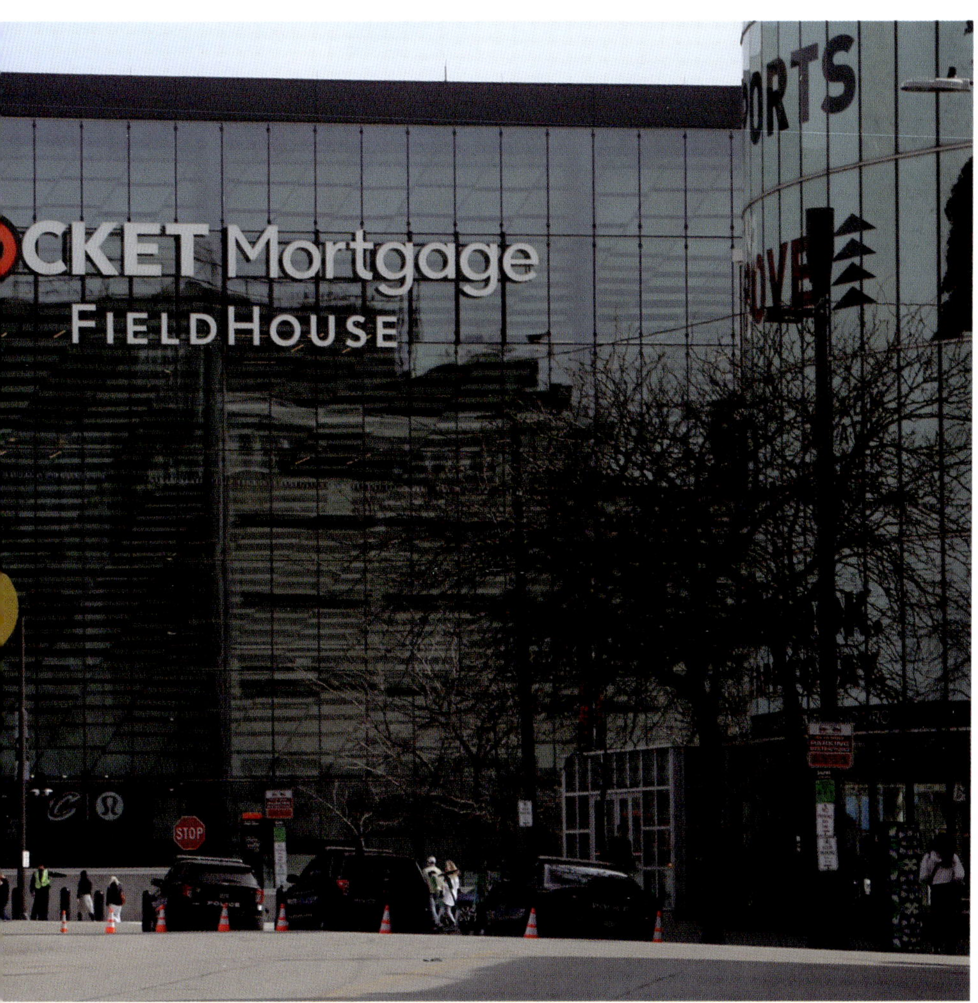

Rocket Arena, home to the Cleveland Cavaliers and Cleveland Monsters

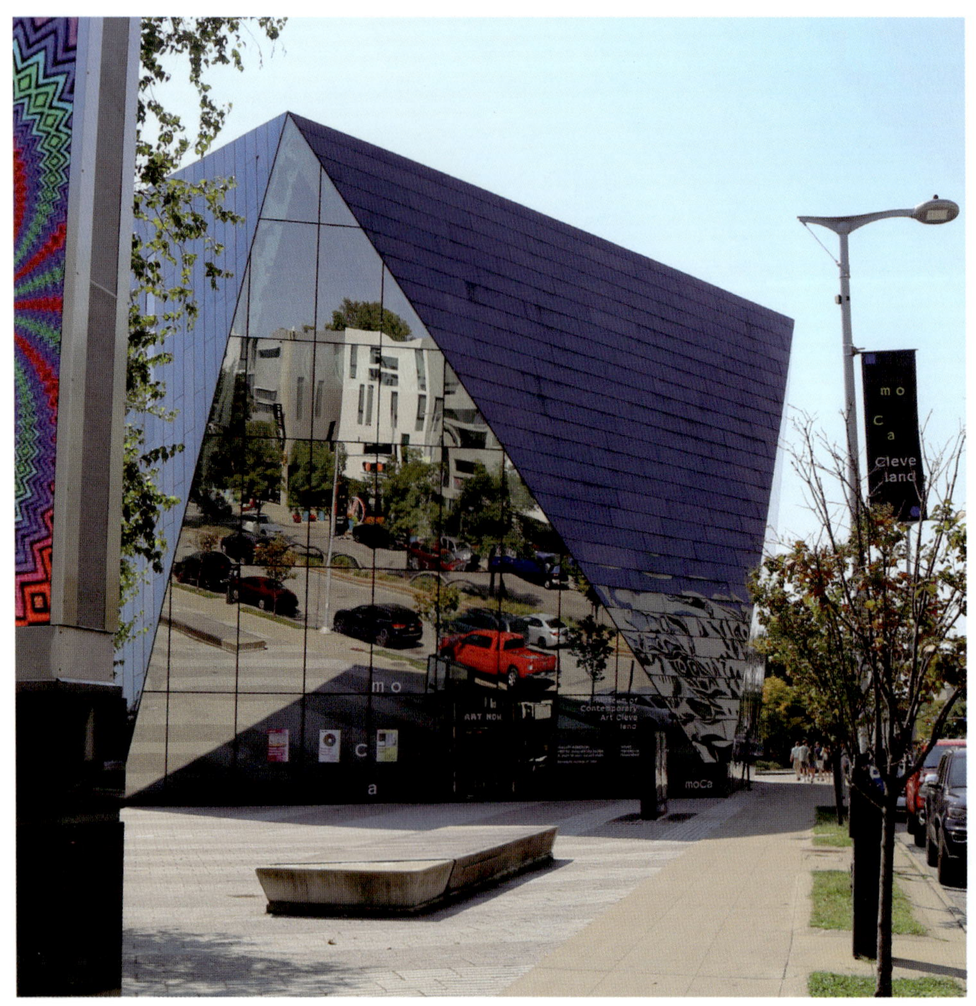

The Museum of Contemporary Art Cleveland

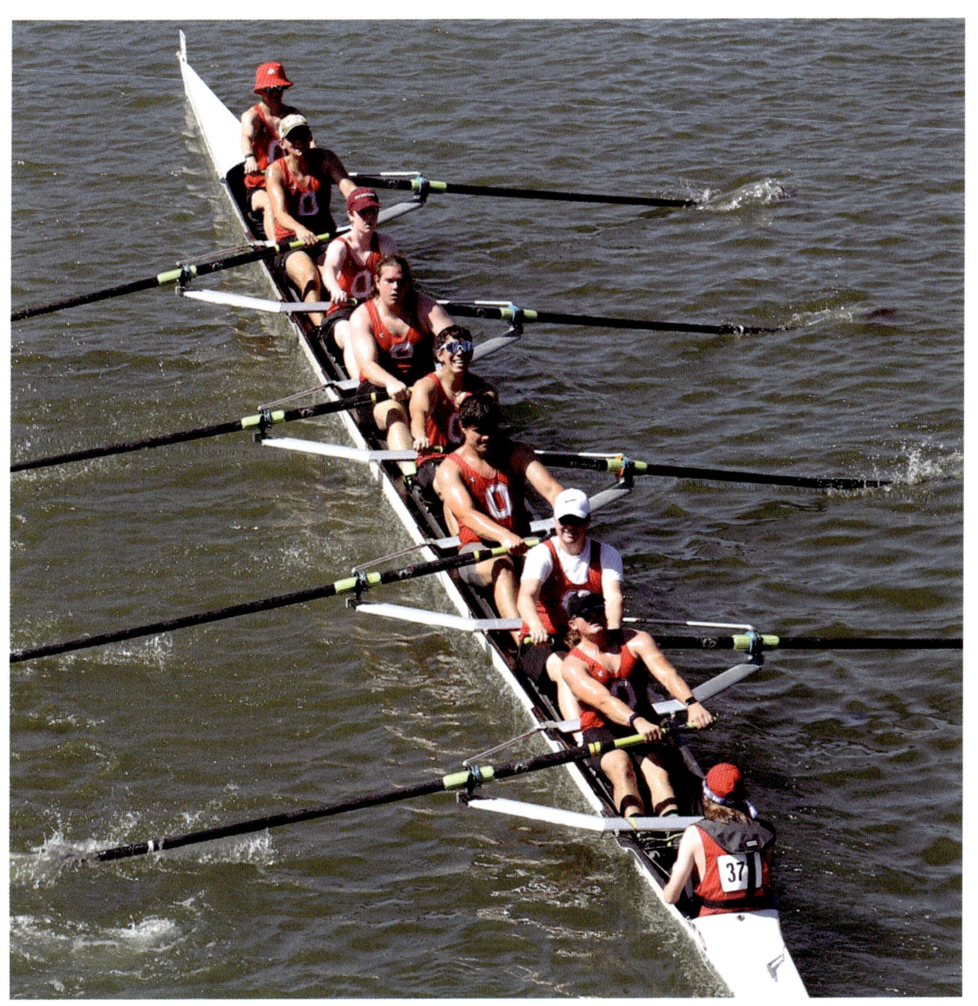

Rowers pulling their way down the Cuyahoga River

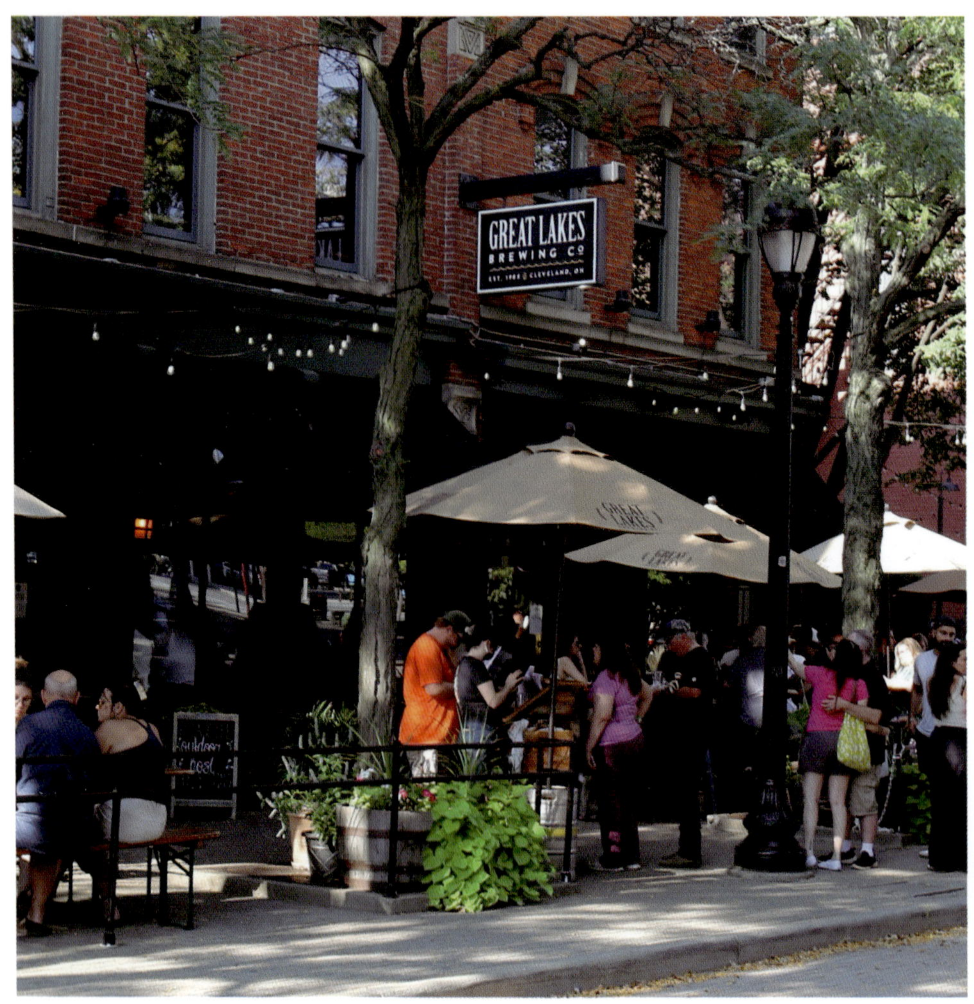

The Great Lakes Brewing Company in Ohio City

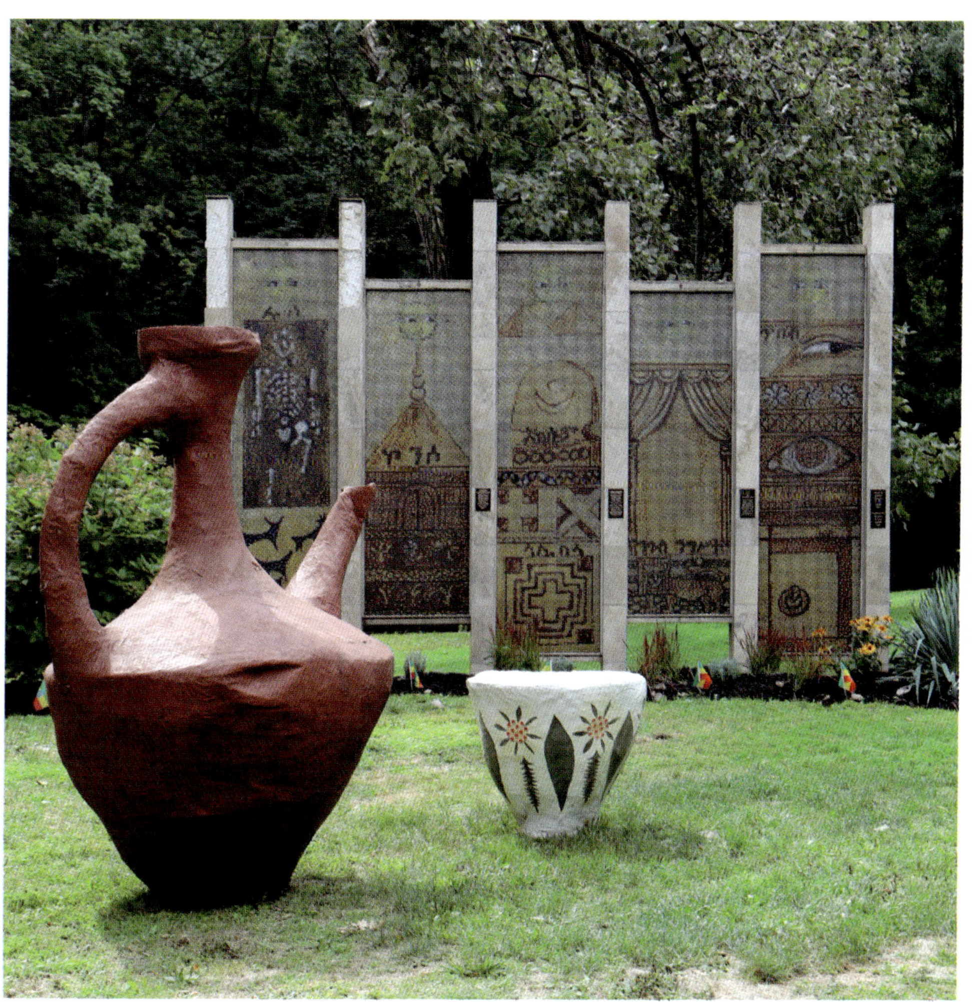

Ethiopian History Mosaic in the Cleveland Cultural Gardens

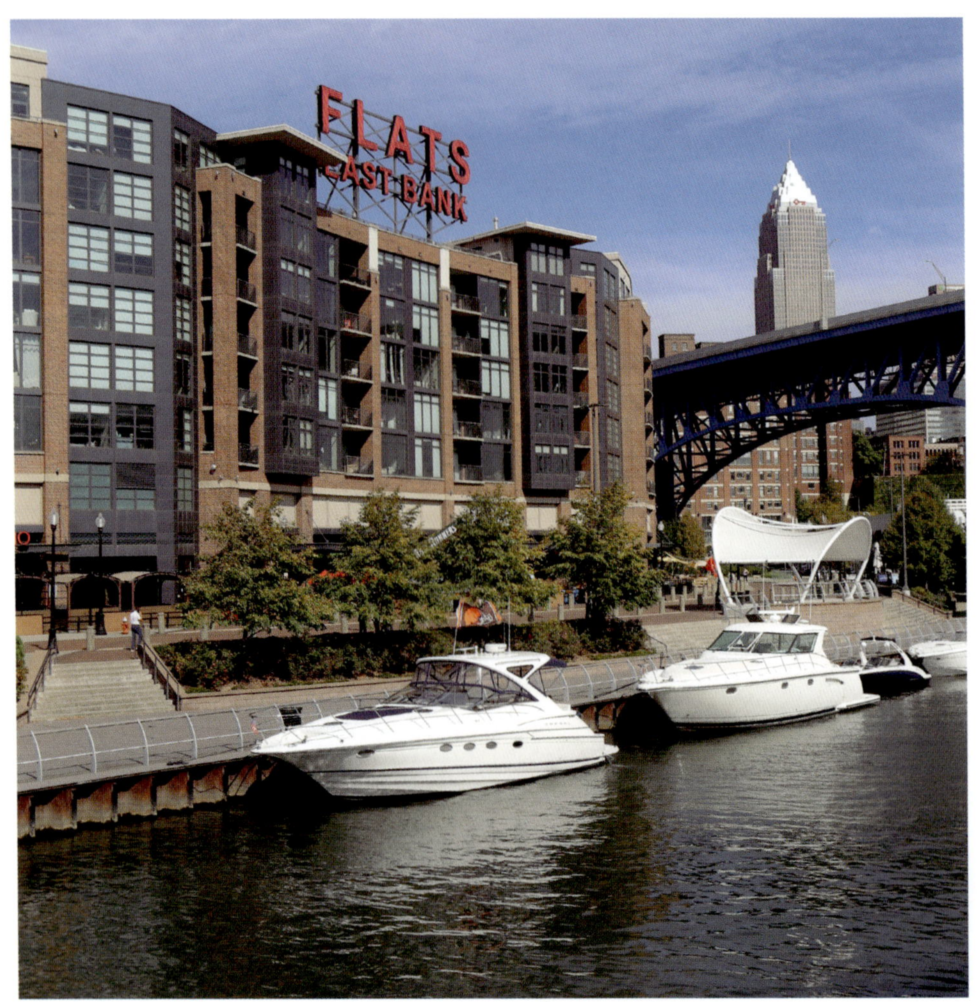

Residential living on the East Bank of the Flats

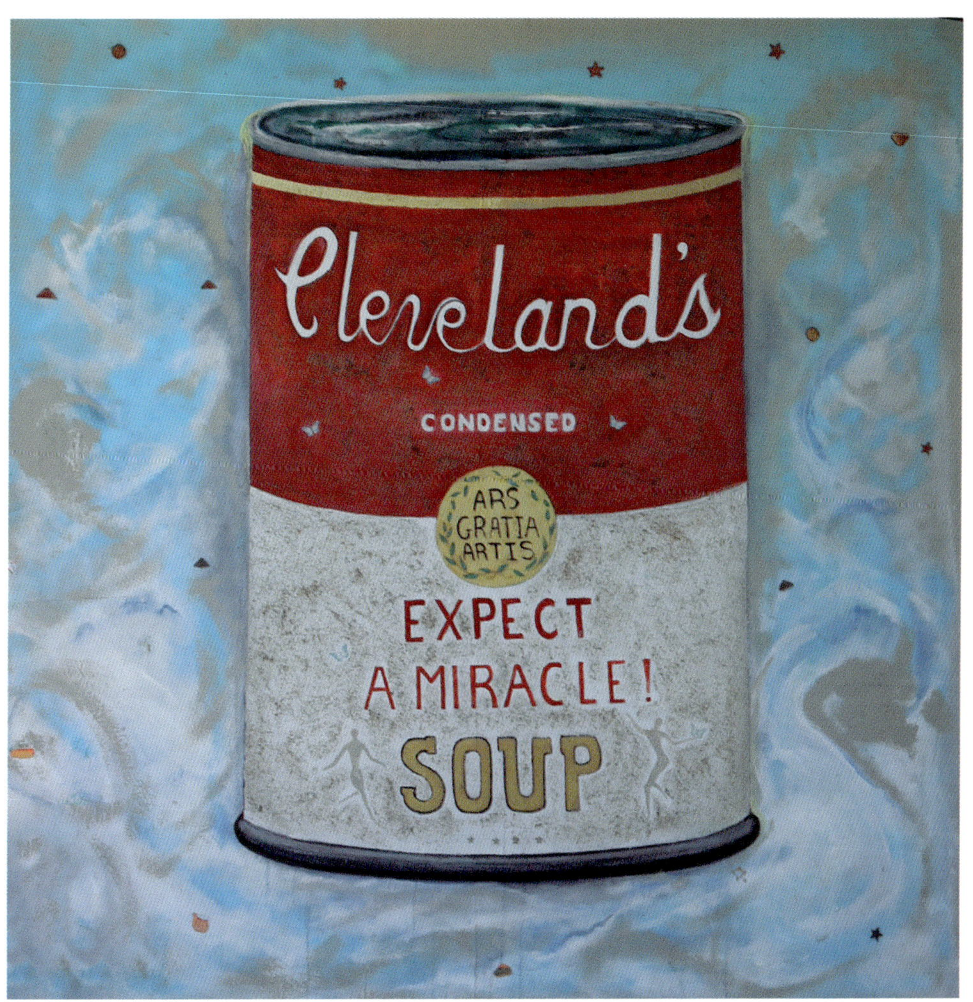

A colorful mural on a building in Tremont

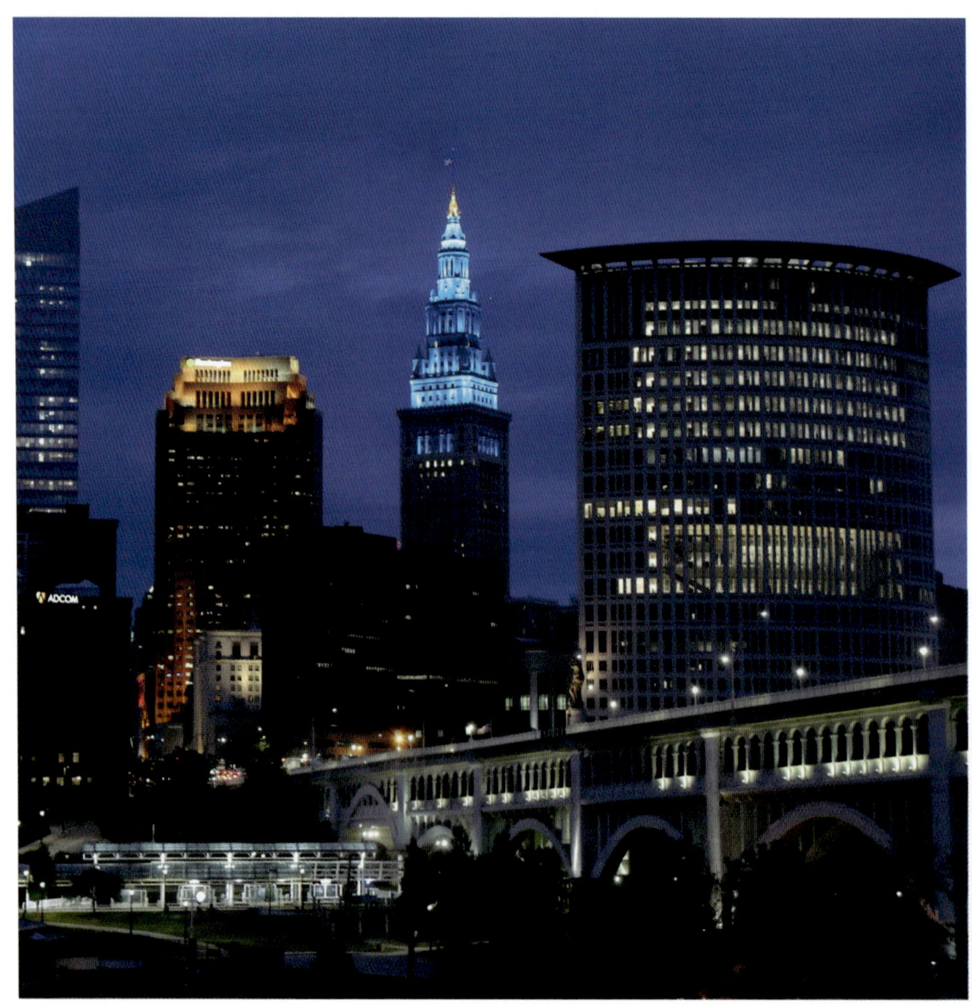

Downtown Cleveland at night

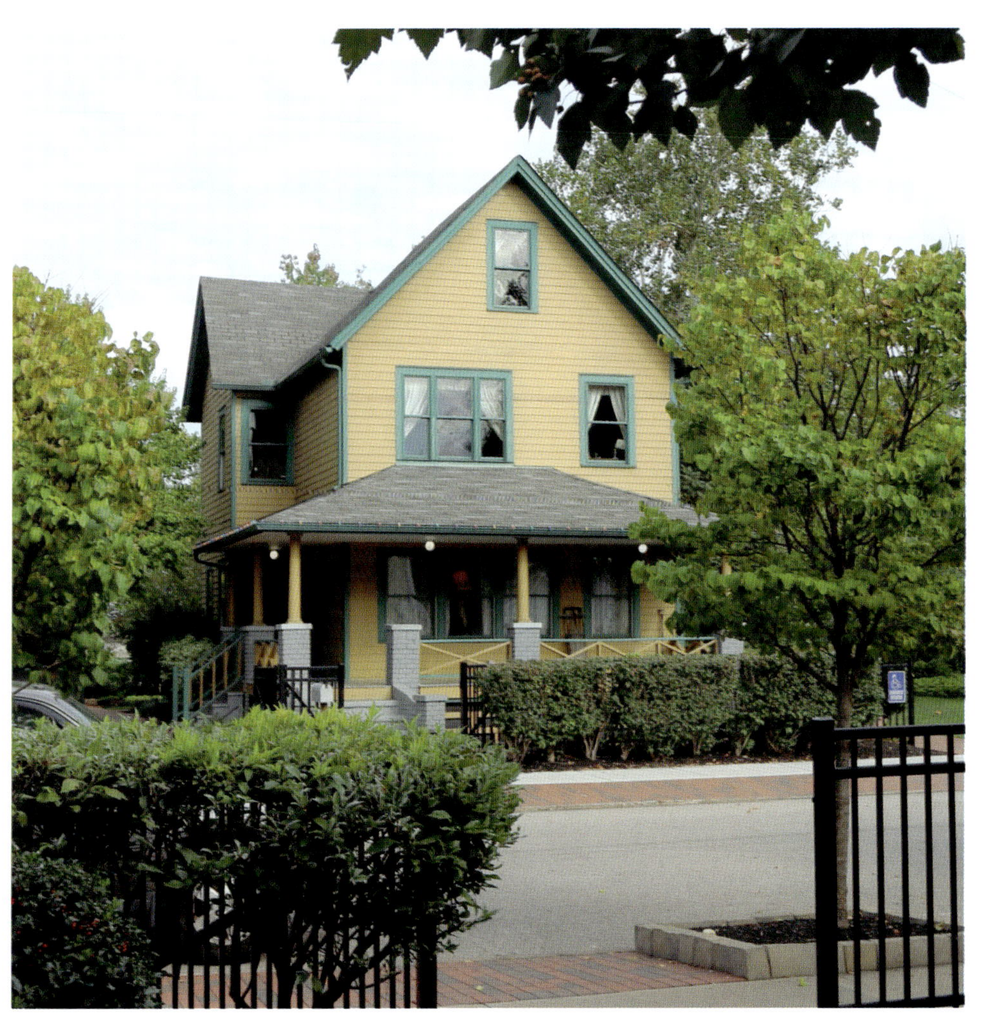

The house from the movie *A Christmas Story*

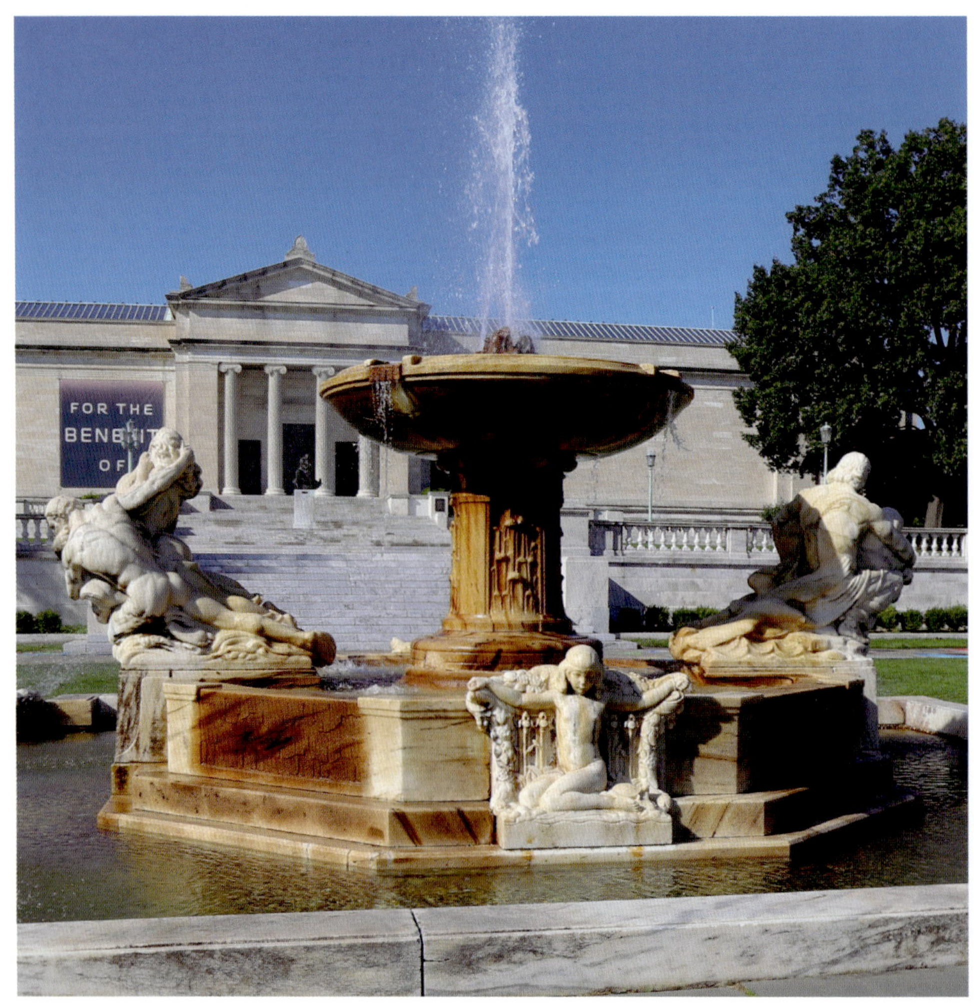

Fountain of the Water, the centerpiece of the Fine Arts Garden

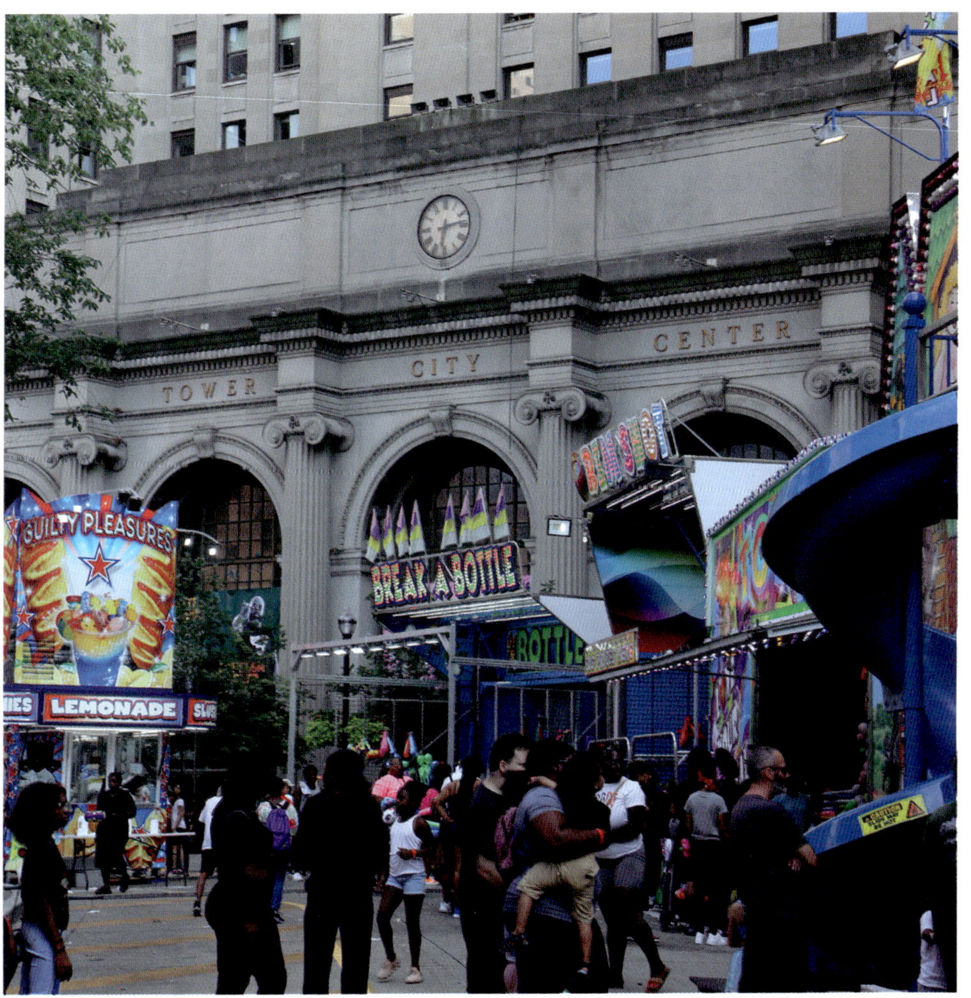

A carnival in Public Square in front of Tower City Center

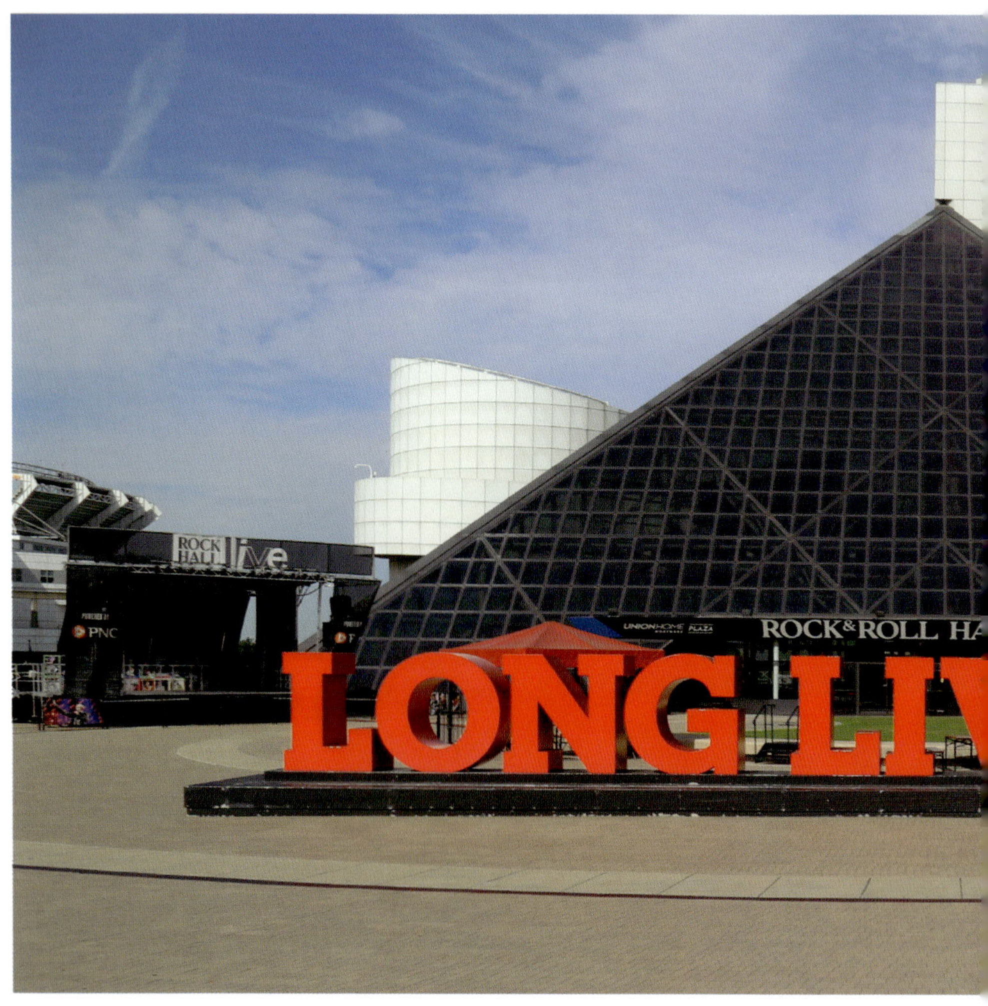
ROCK HALL live
PNC
UNION HOME PLAZA
ROCK&ROLL HA
LONG LIV

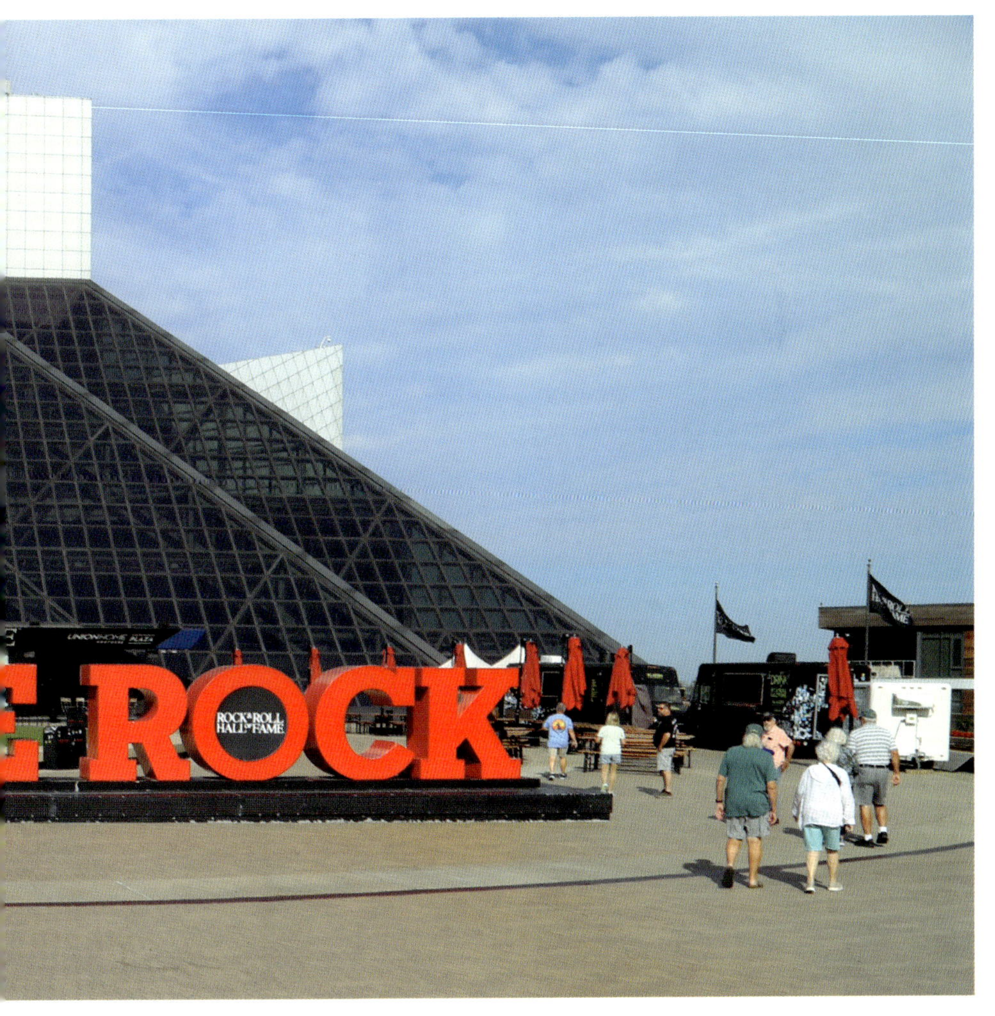

The Rock & Roll Hall of Fame in downtown Cleveland

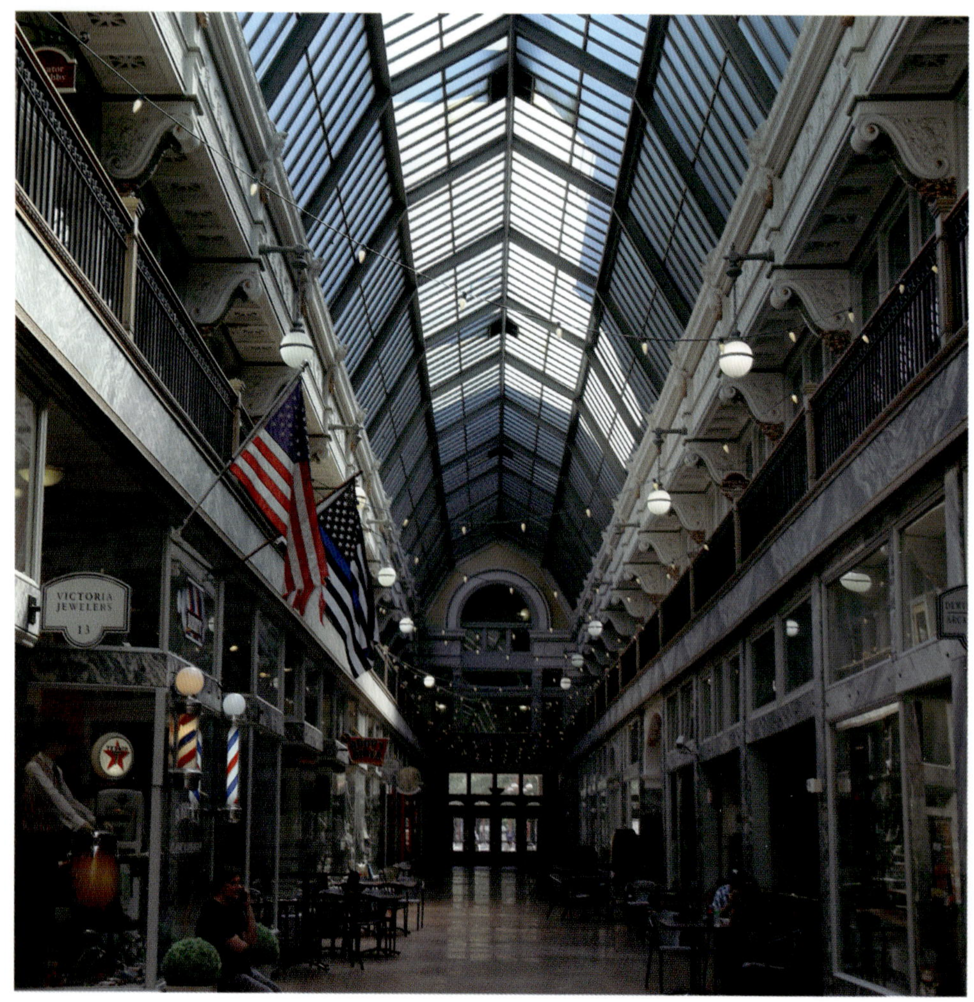

The historic 5th Street Arcades

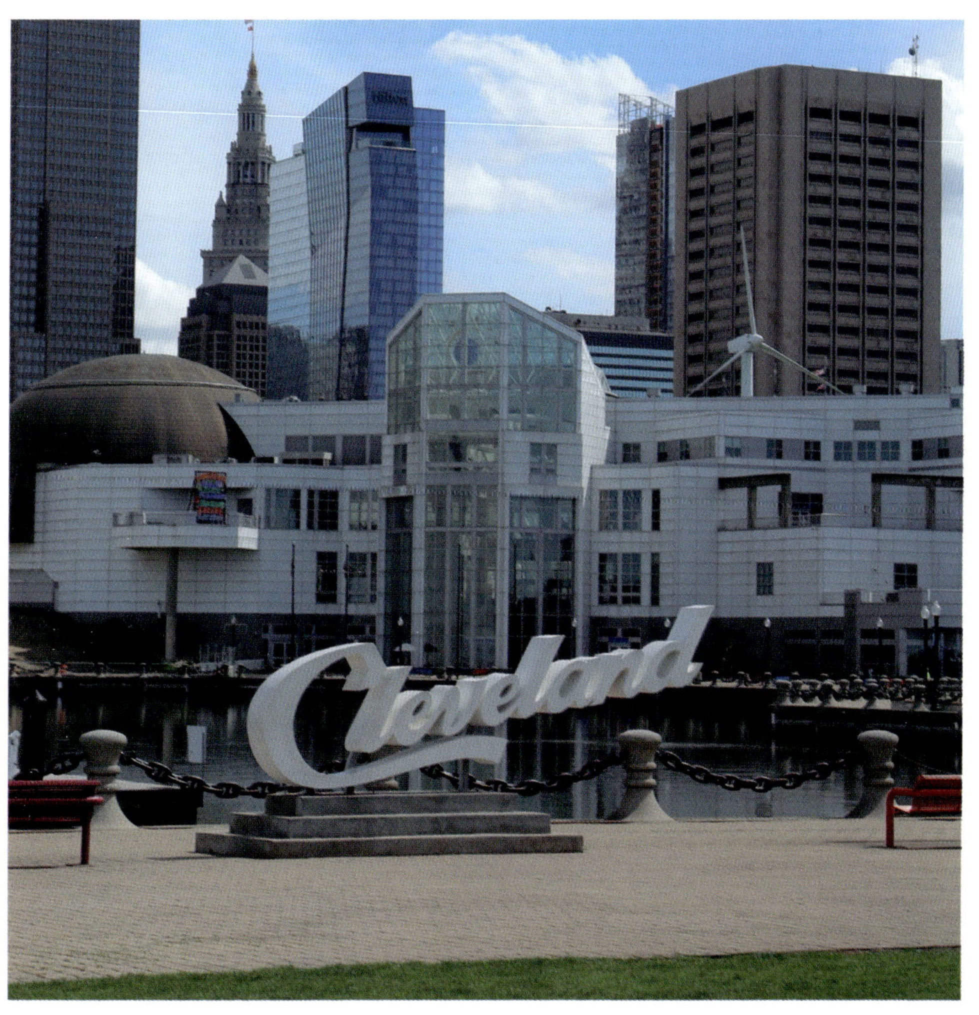

The Cleveland Script Sign located at the North Coast Harbor

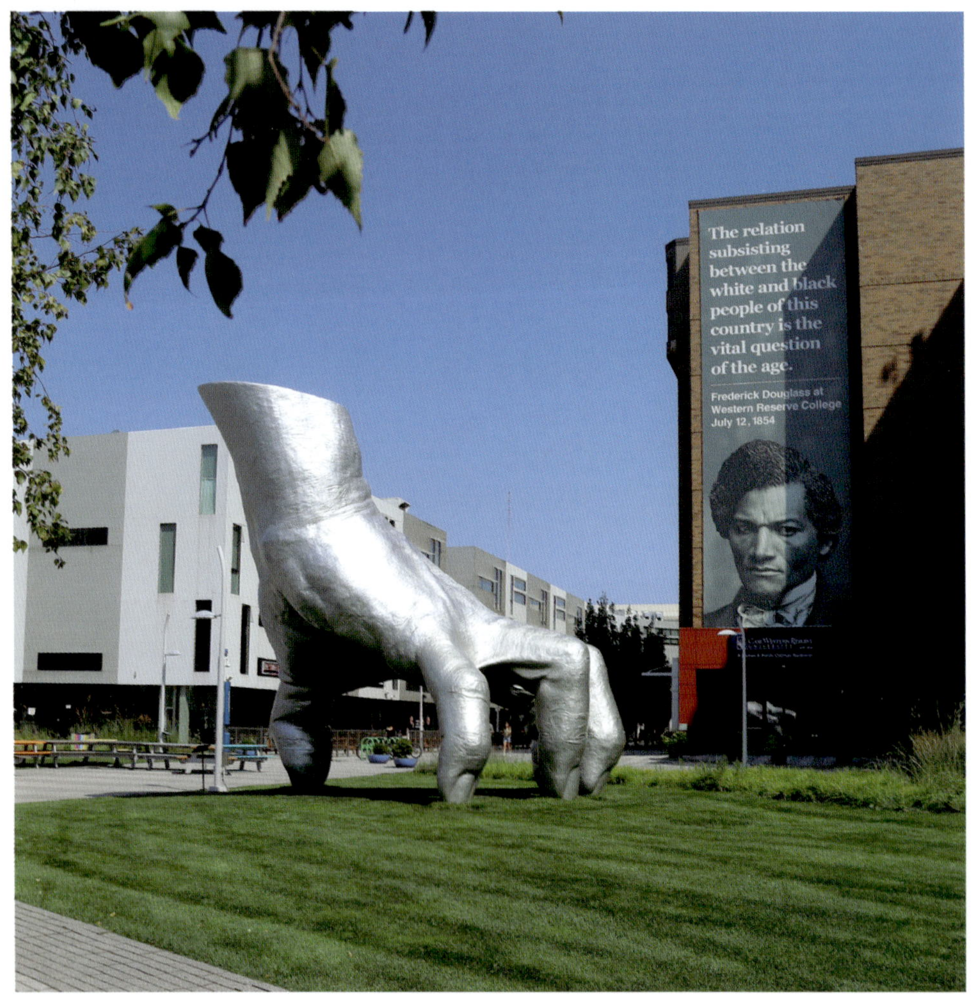

Judy's Hand Pavilion outside MOCA

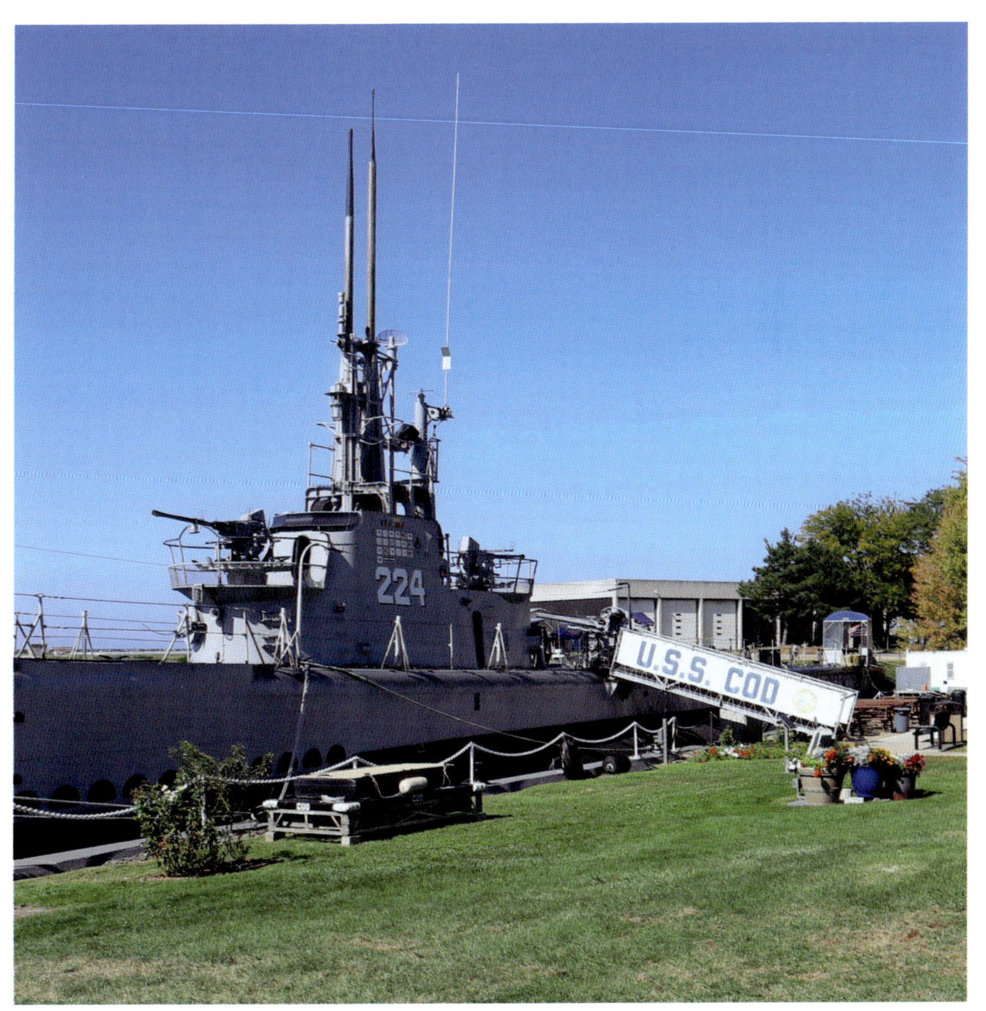

The USS *Cod* Submarine Memorial is a must-visit.

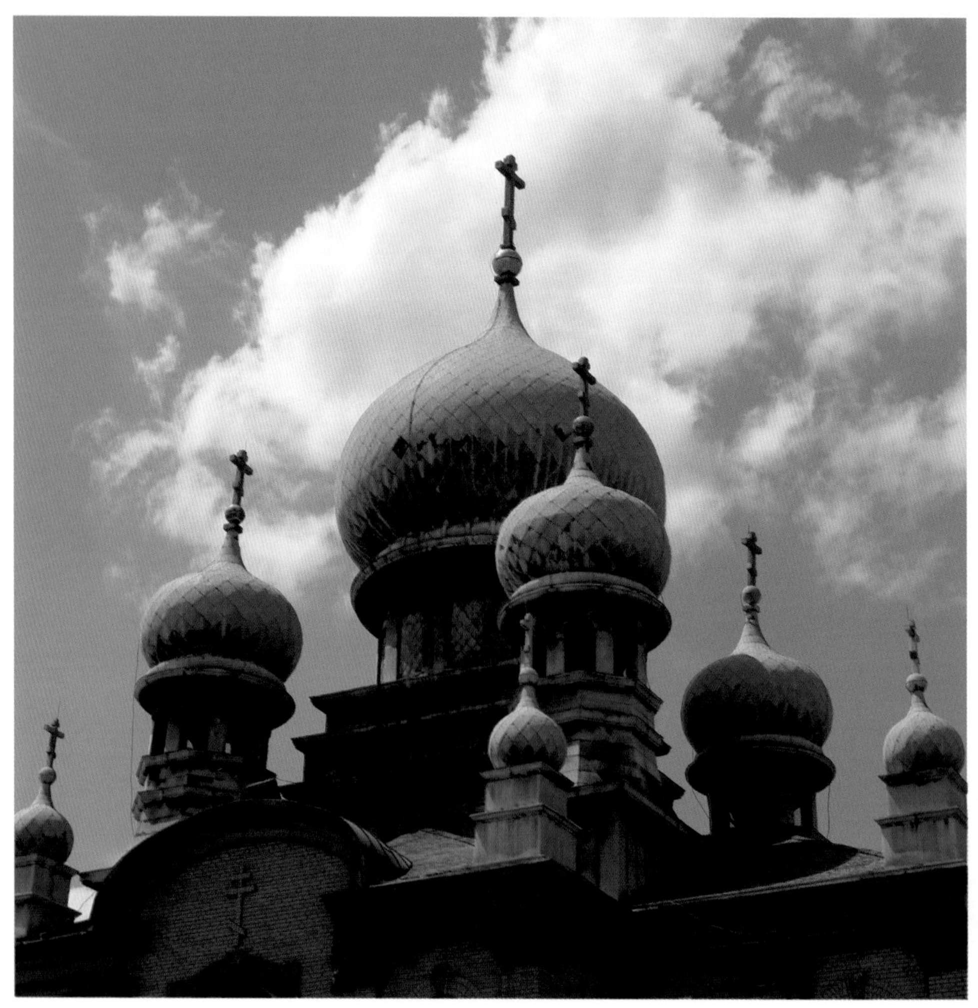

St. Theodosius Orthodox Cathedral was featured in the movie *The Deer Hunter*.

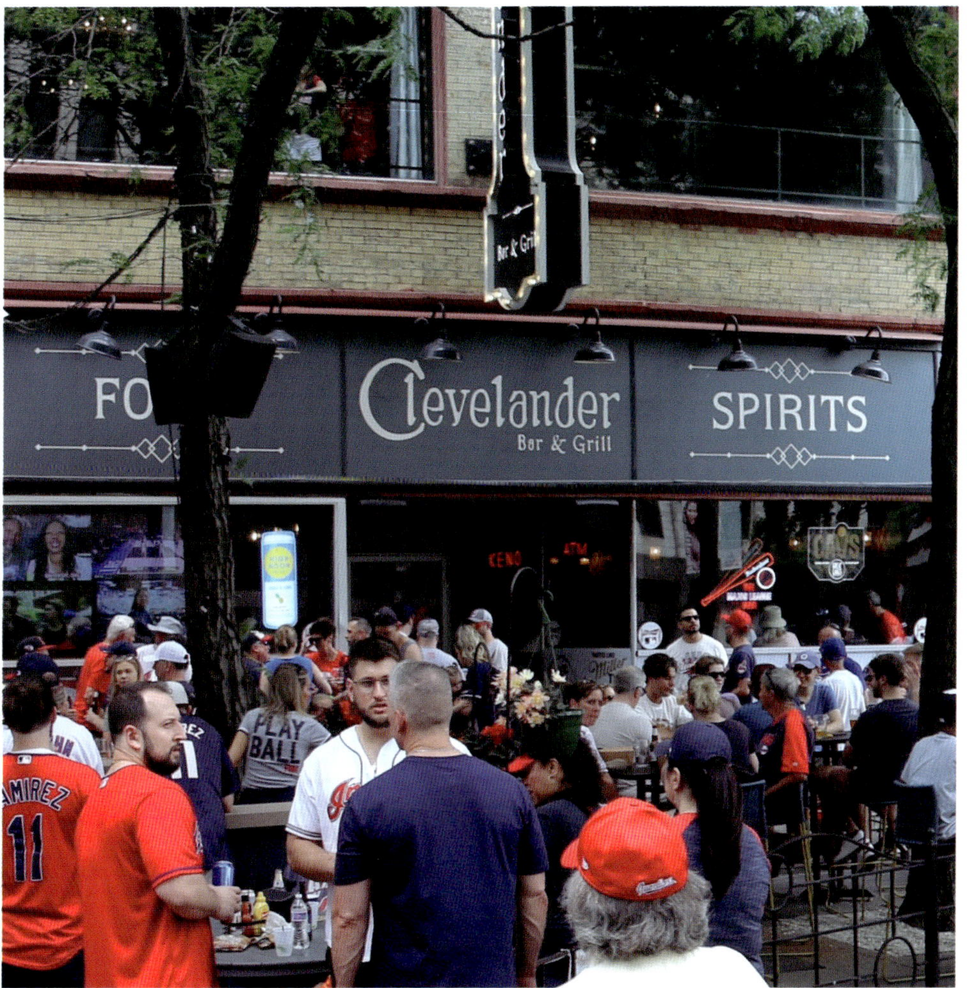

The Clevelander Bar & Grill, CLE's favorite sports bar

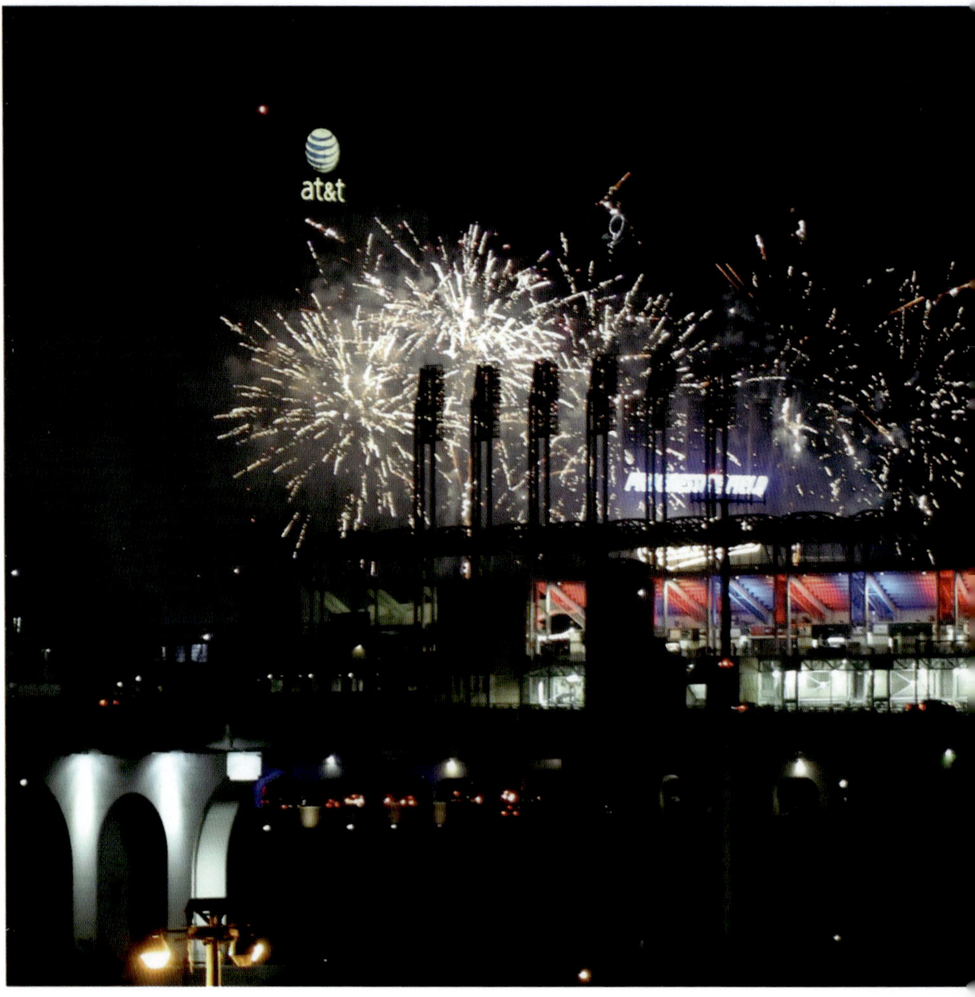
at&t

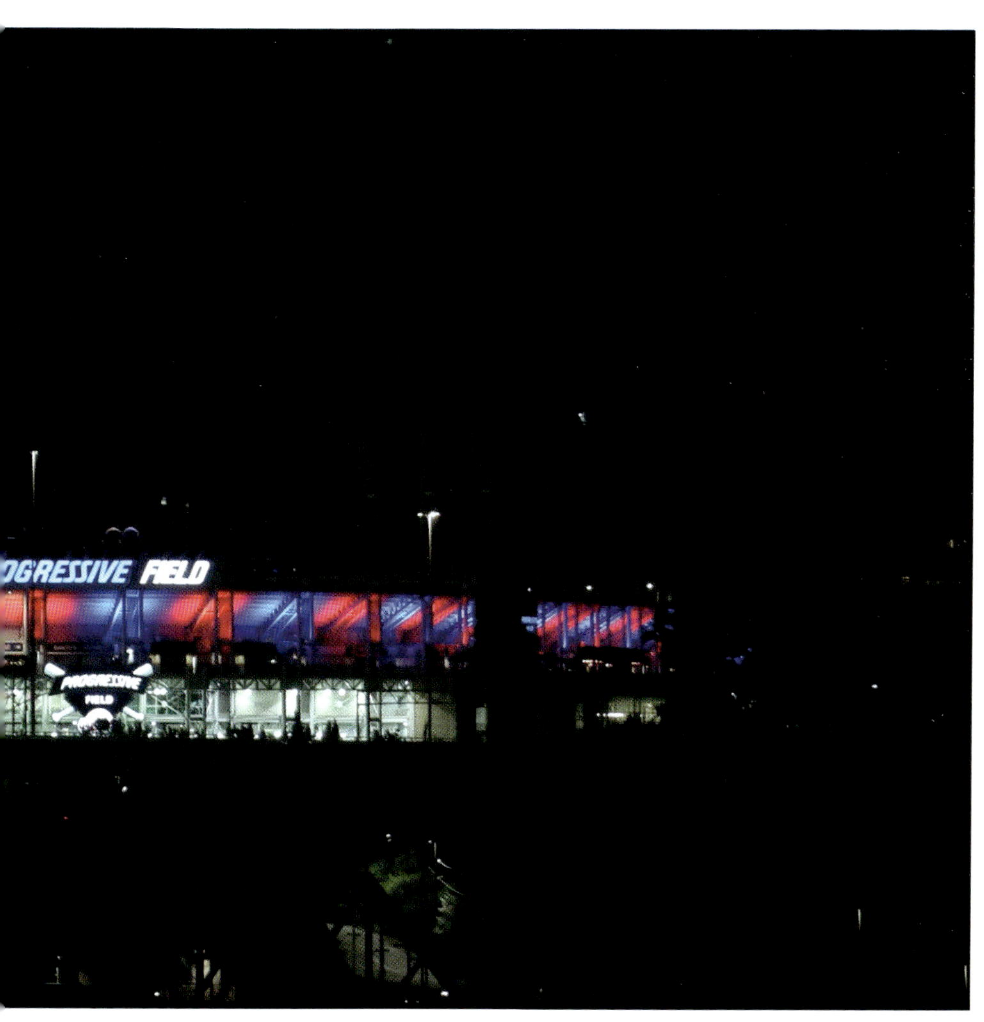

Fireworks to celebrate another Guardians victory at Progressive Field

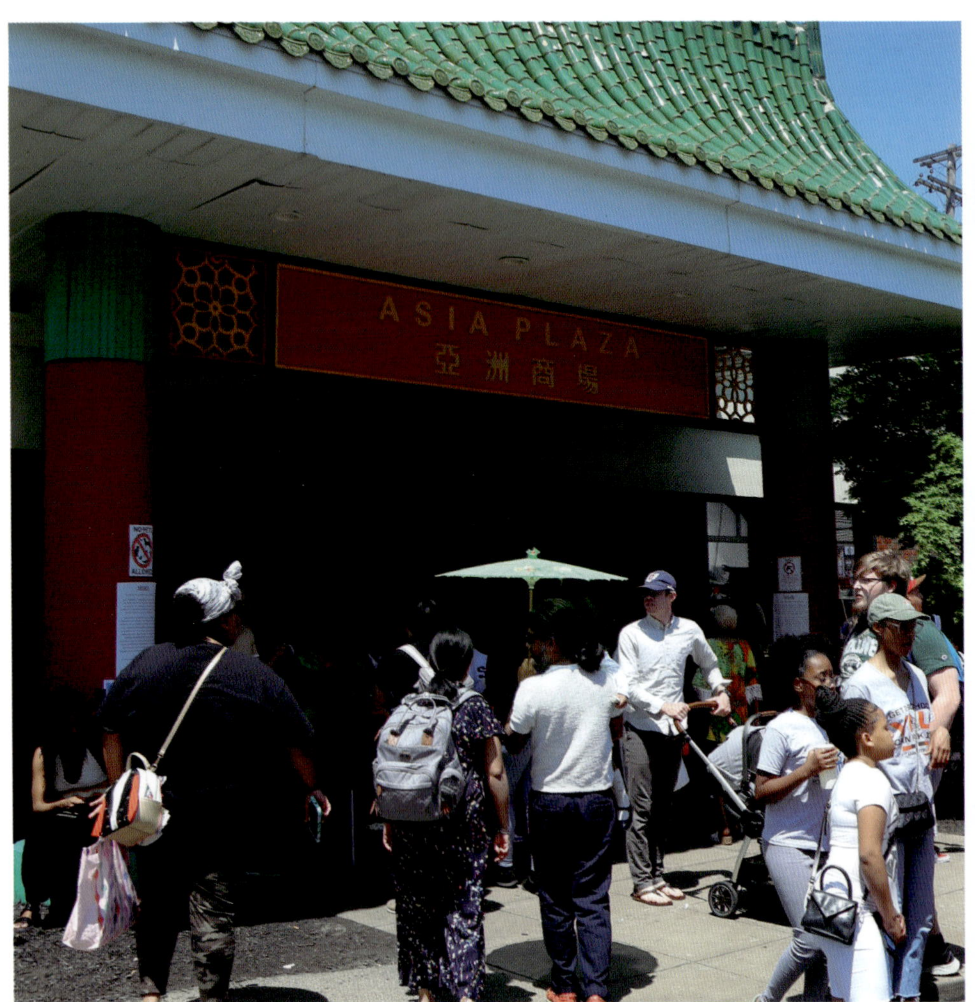

Asia Plaza is the heart of Cleveland's AsiaTown.

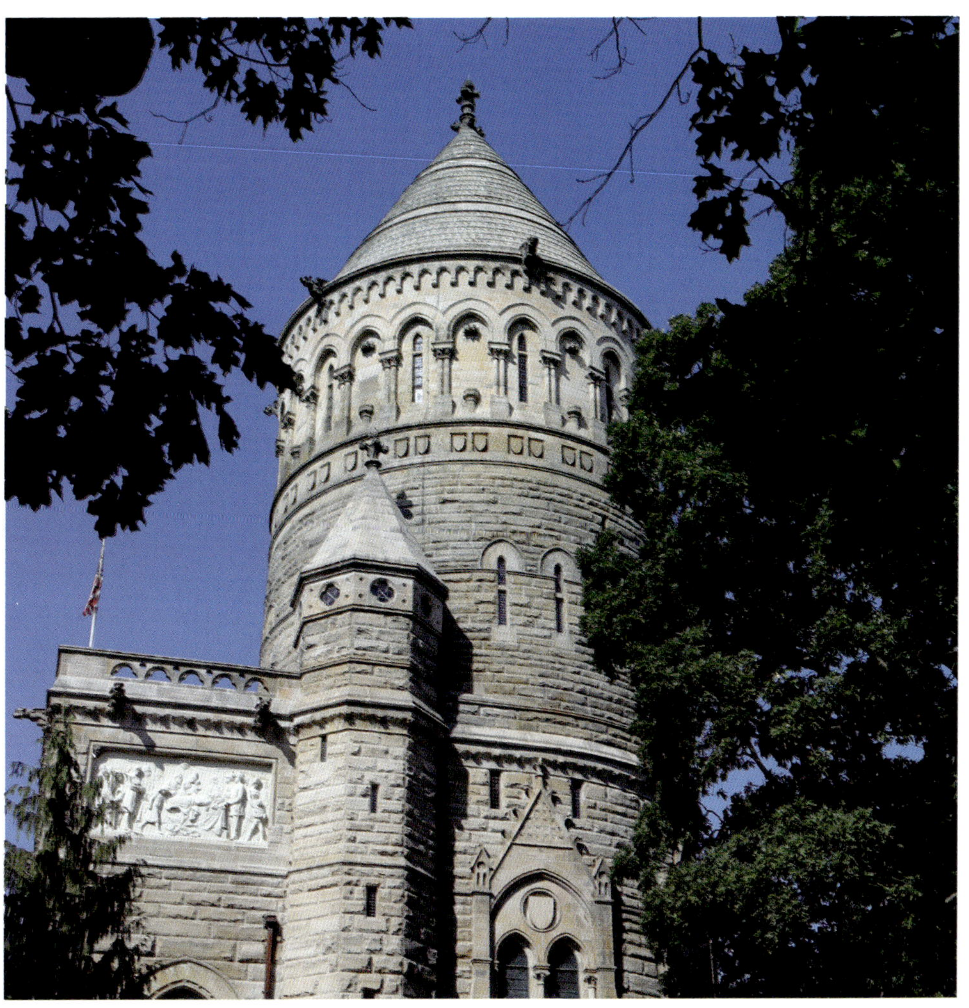

The top of the President James A. Garfield Memorial in Lake View Cemetery

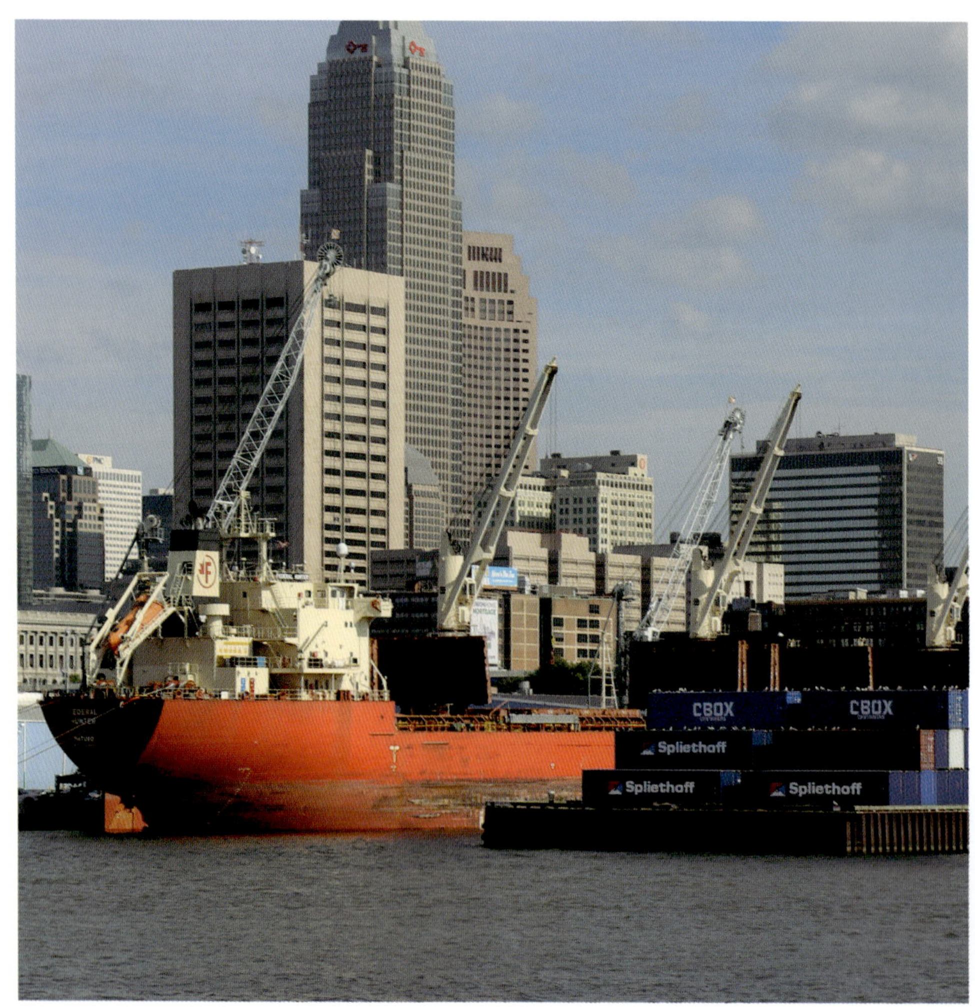

A cargo freighter unloads at the Port of Cleveland.

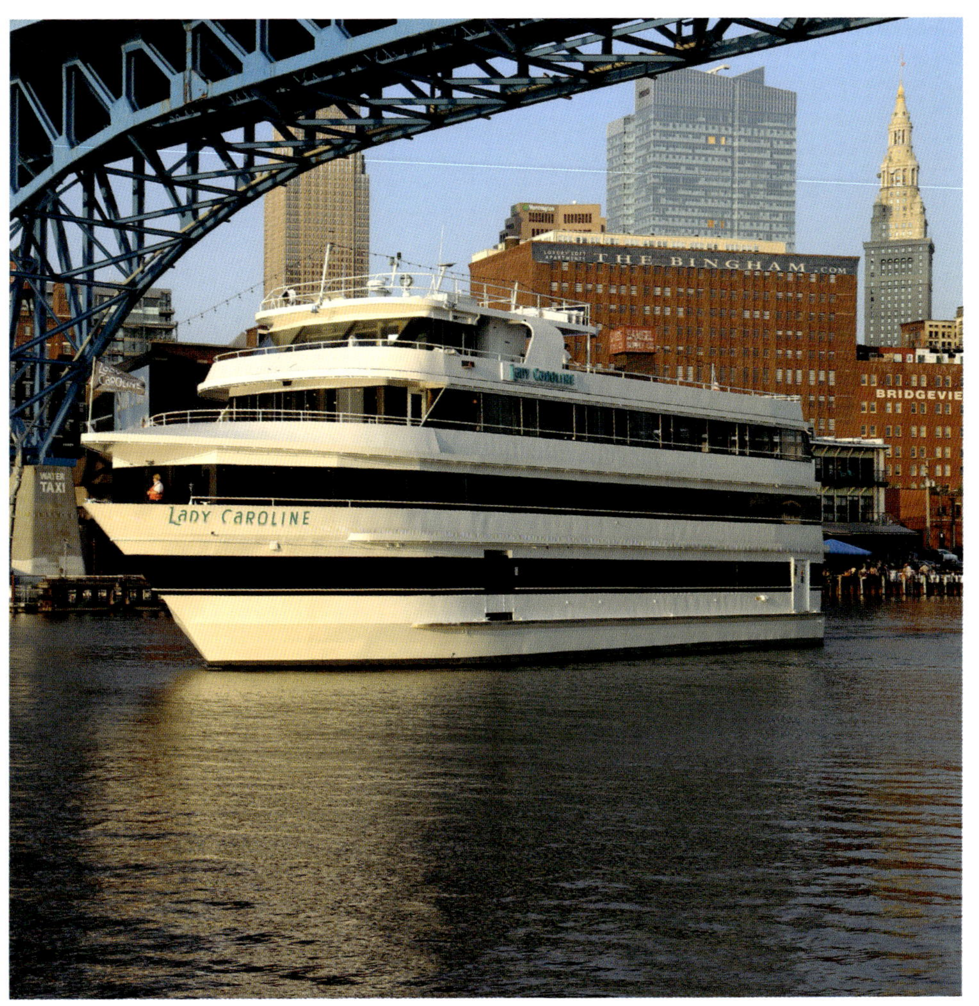

Lady Caroline cruises toward Lake Erie.

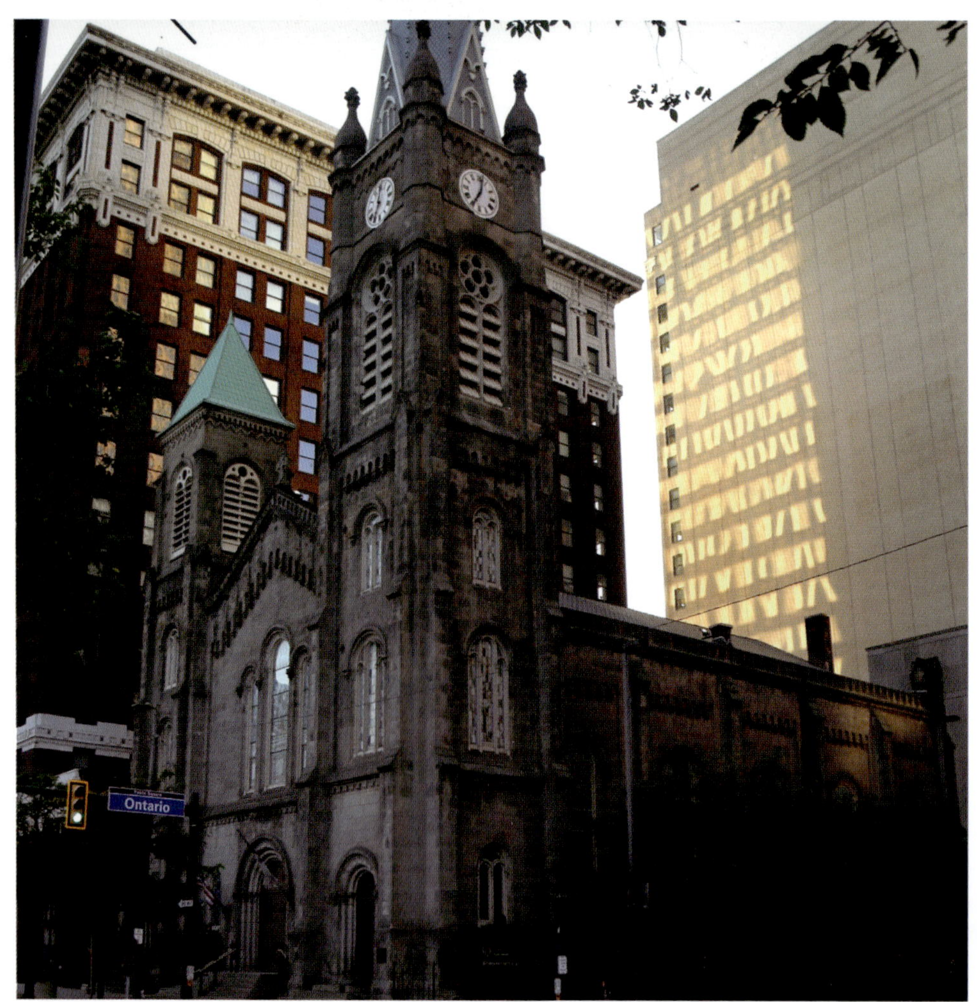

The Old Stone Church overlooks Public Square.

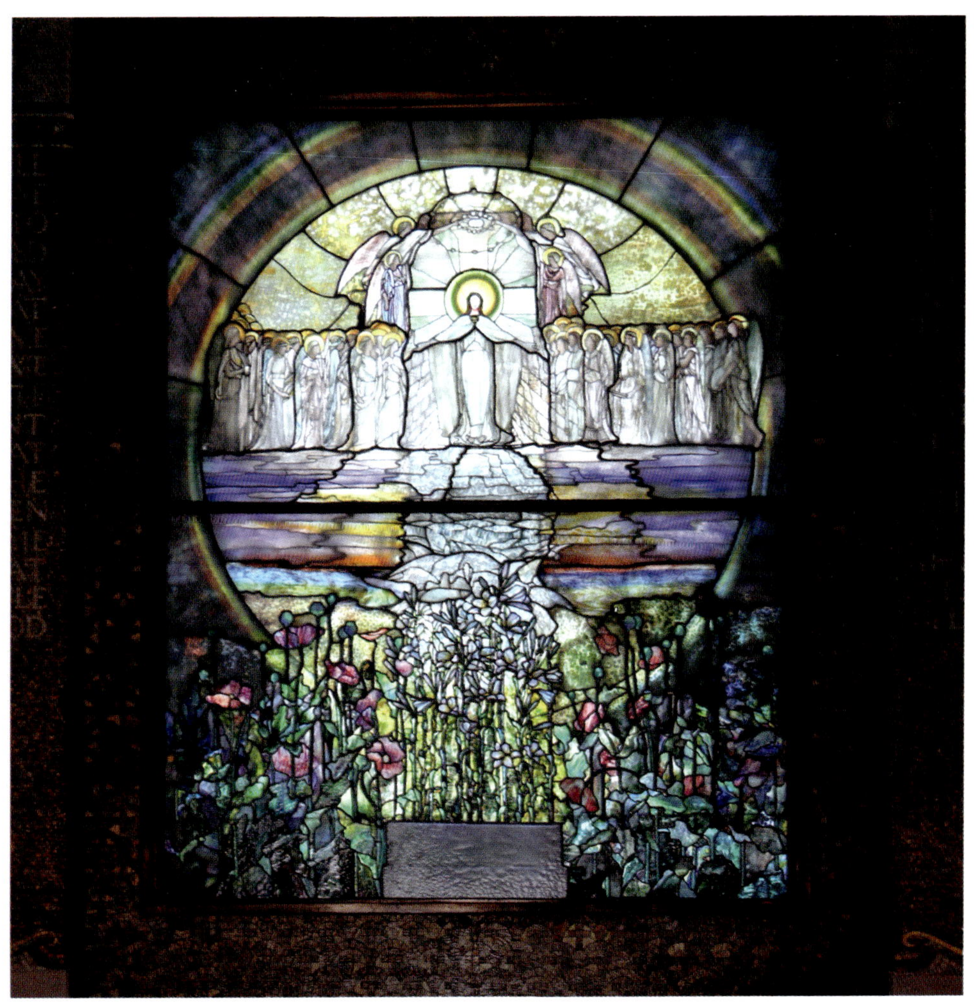

Tiffany's stained-glass window *The Flight of Souls* graces Wade Chapel.

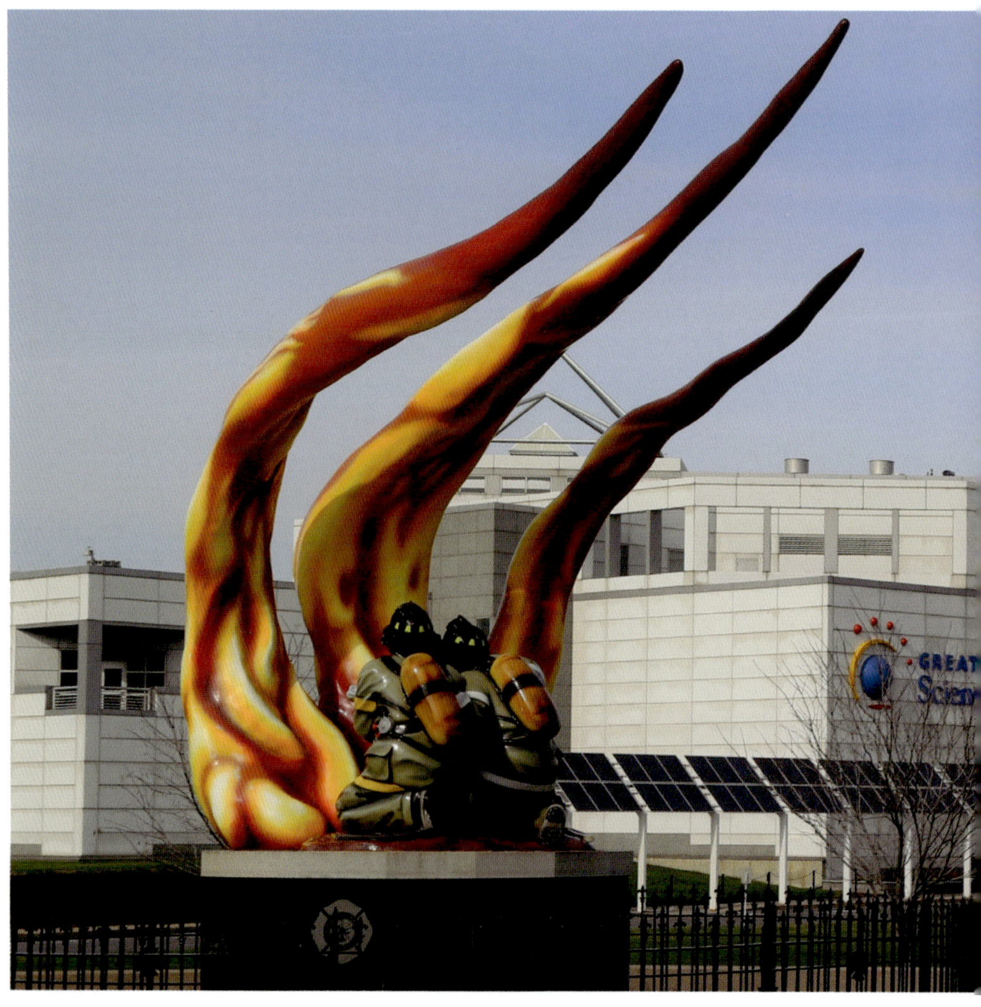

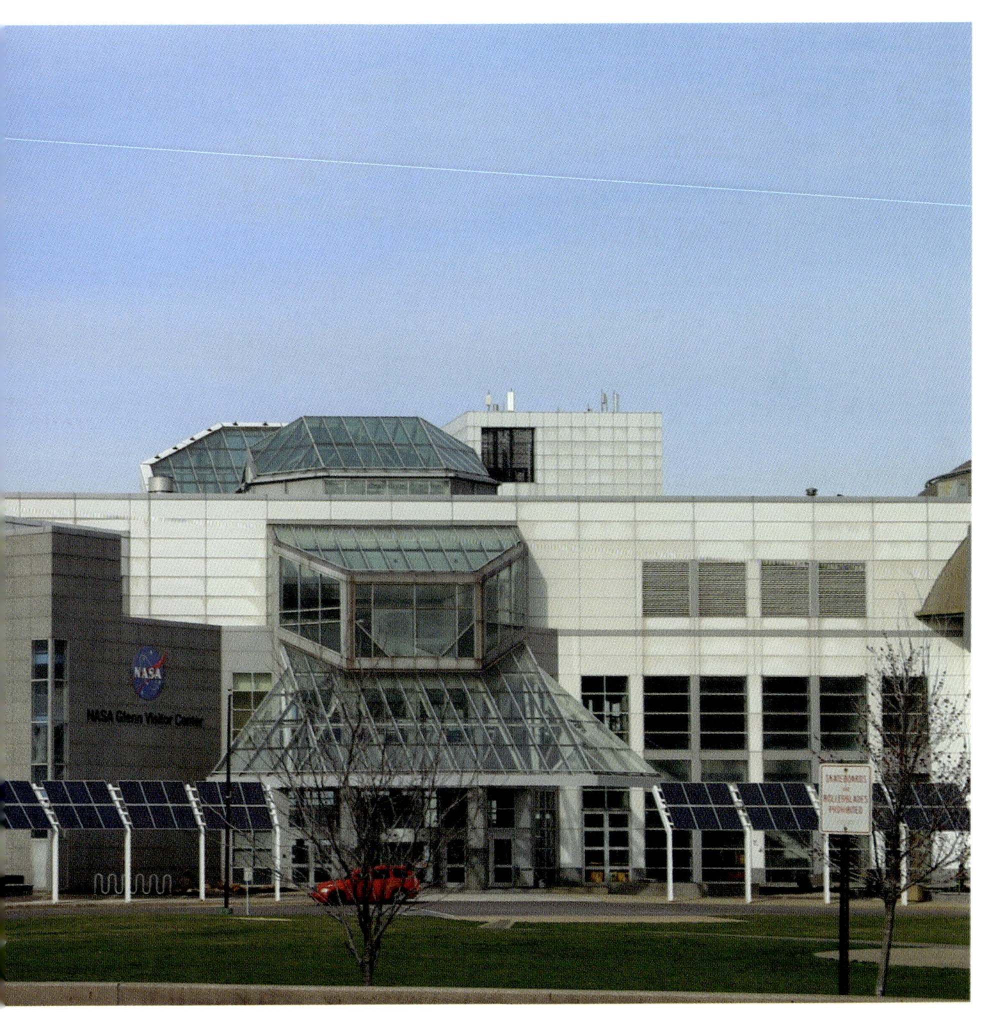

Cleveland Fire Fighters Memorial outside the Great Lakes Science Center

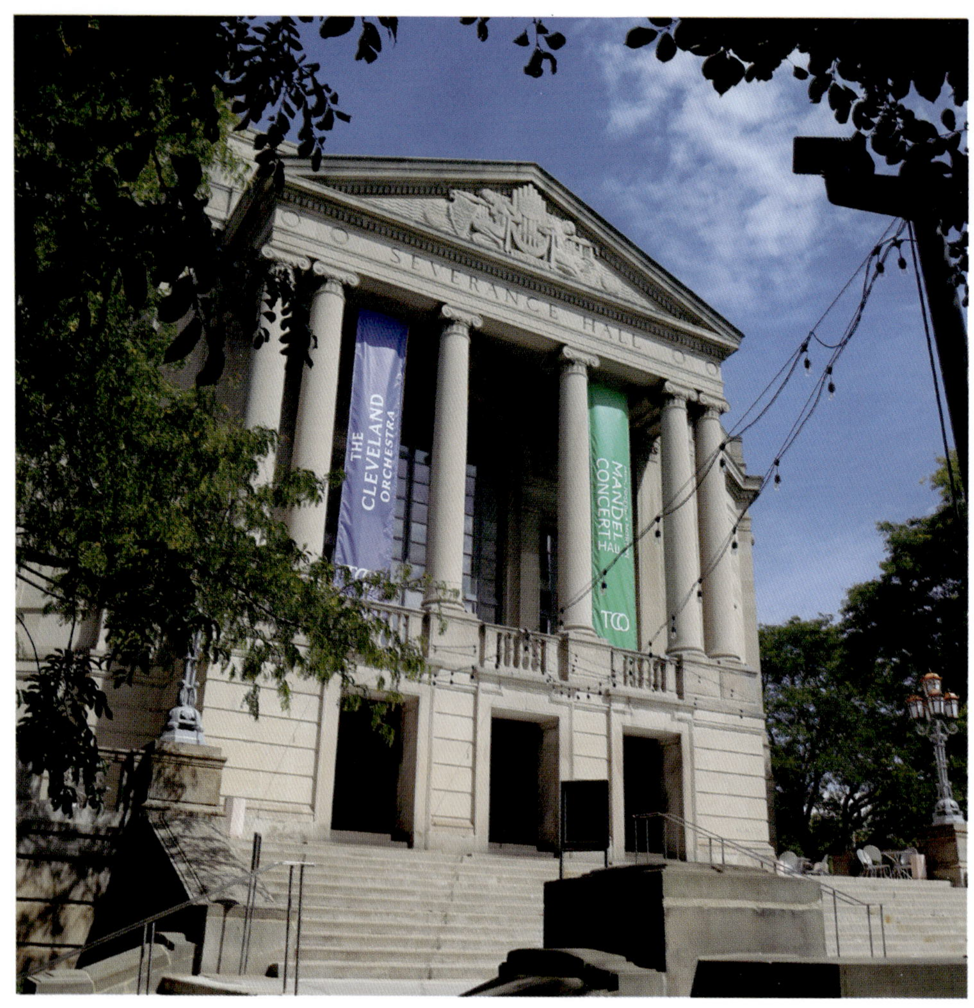

Historic Severance Hall, home to the world-renowned Cleveland Orchestra

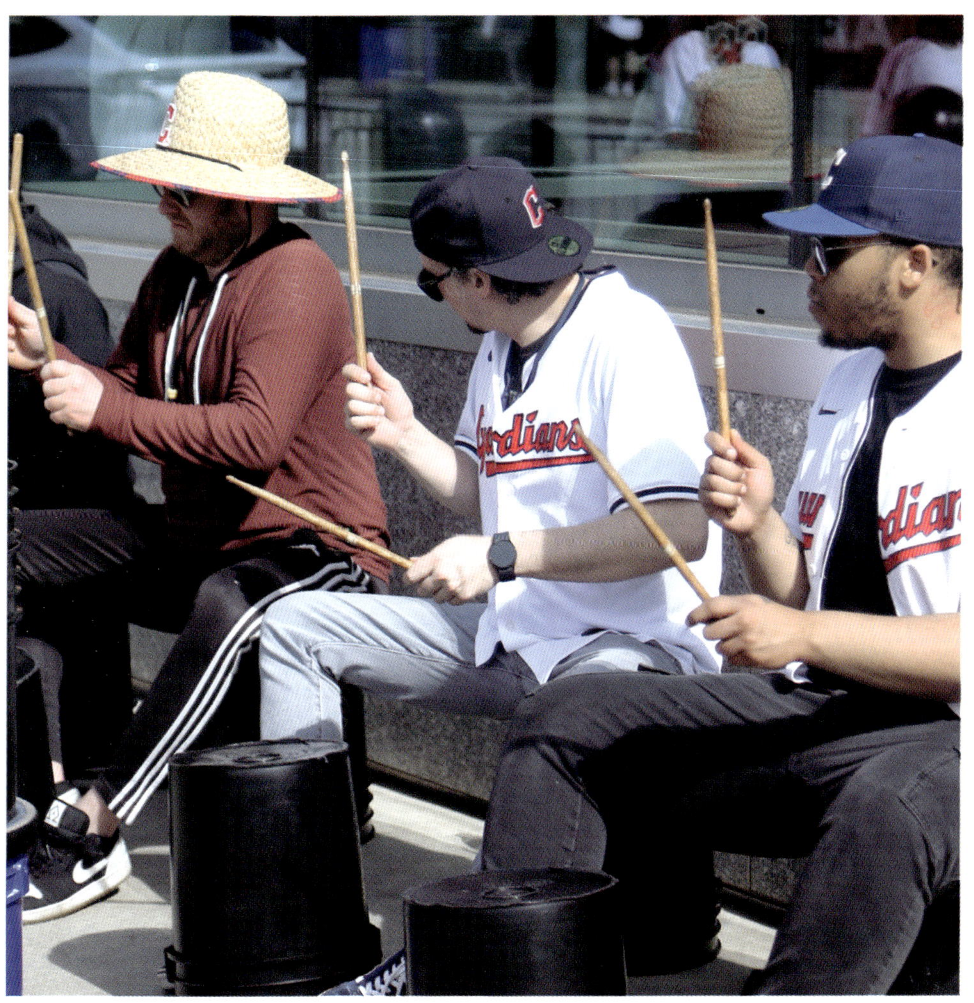

Street drummers entertaining the crowds headed to the Guardians game

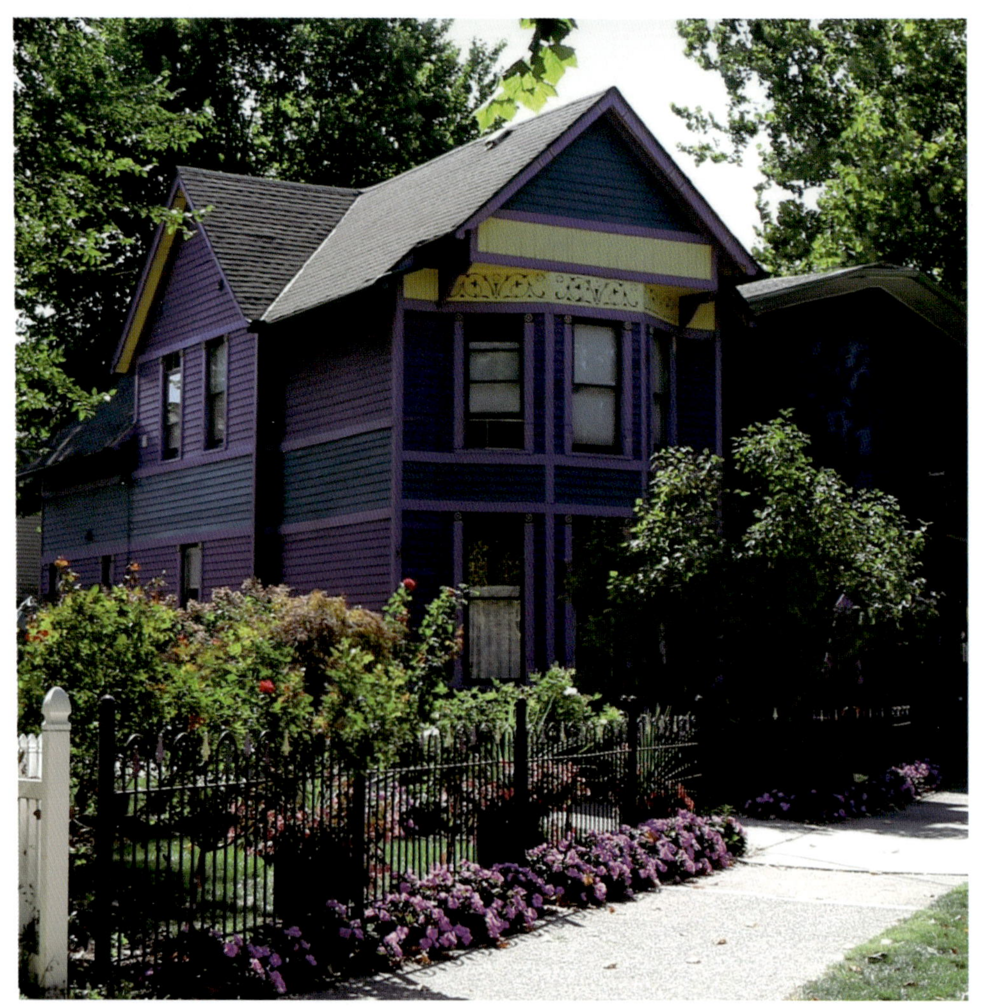

Colorful Victorian homes can be found throughout CLE's neighborhoods.

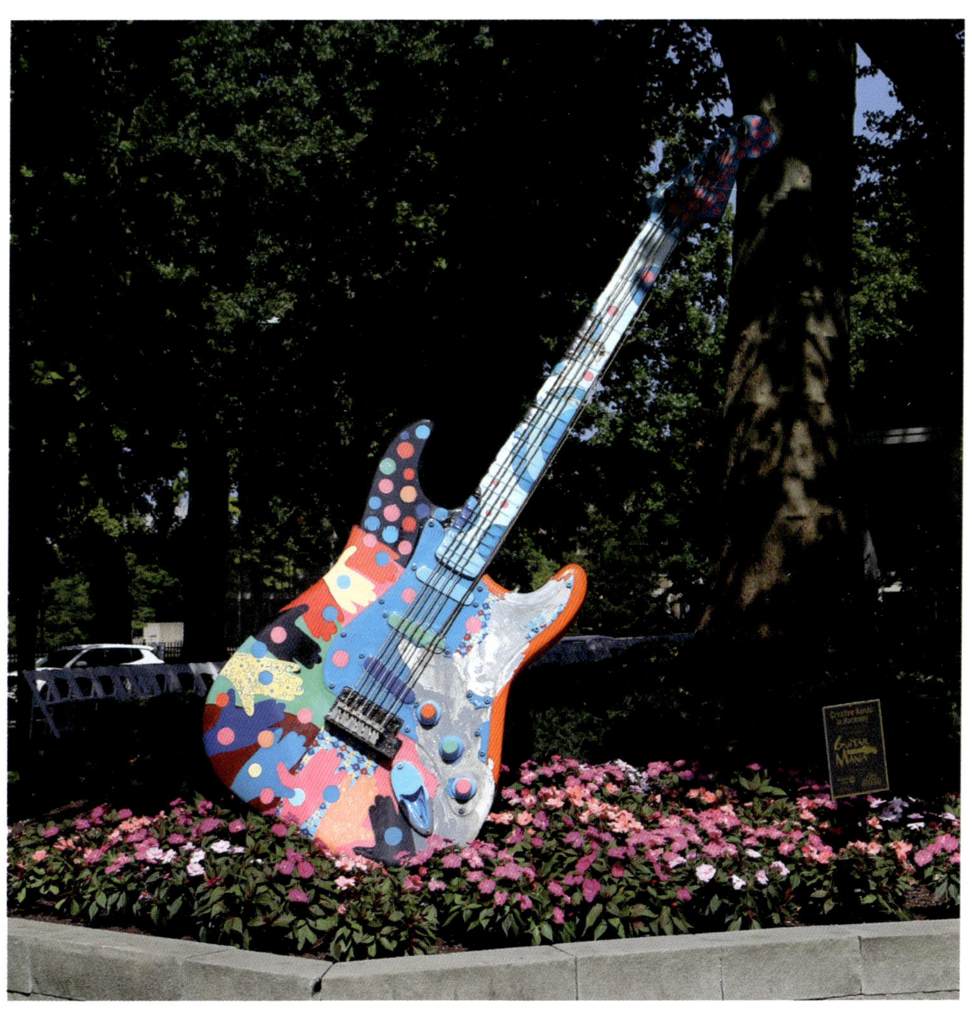

Decorated replicas of Fender Stratocasters can be seen throughout "The Land."

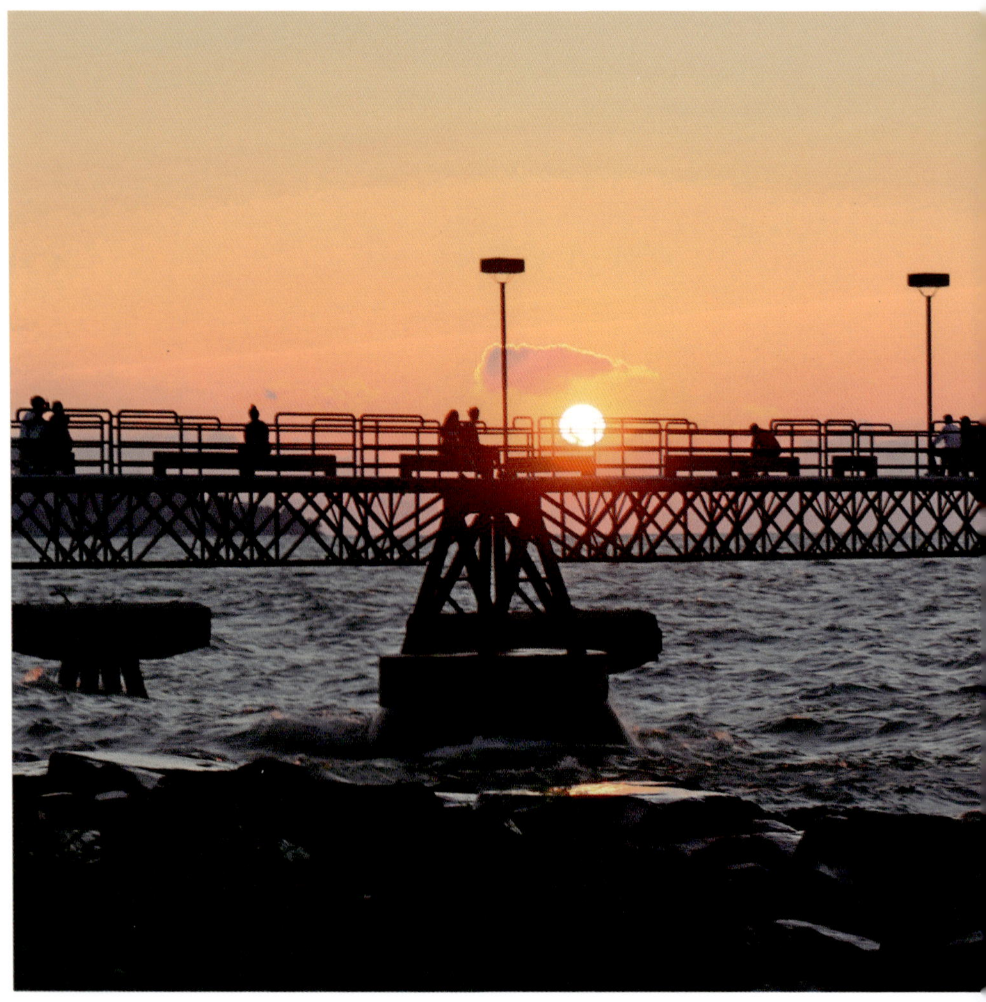

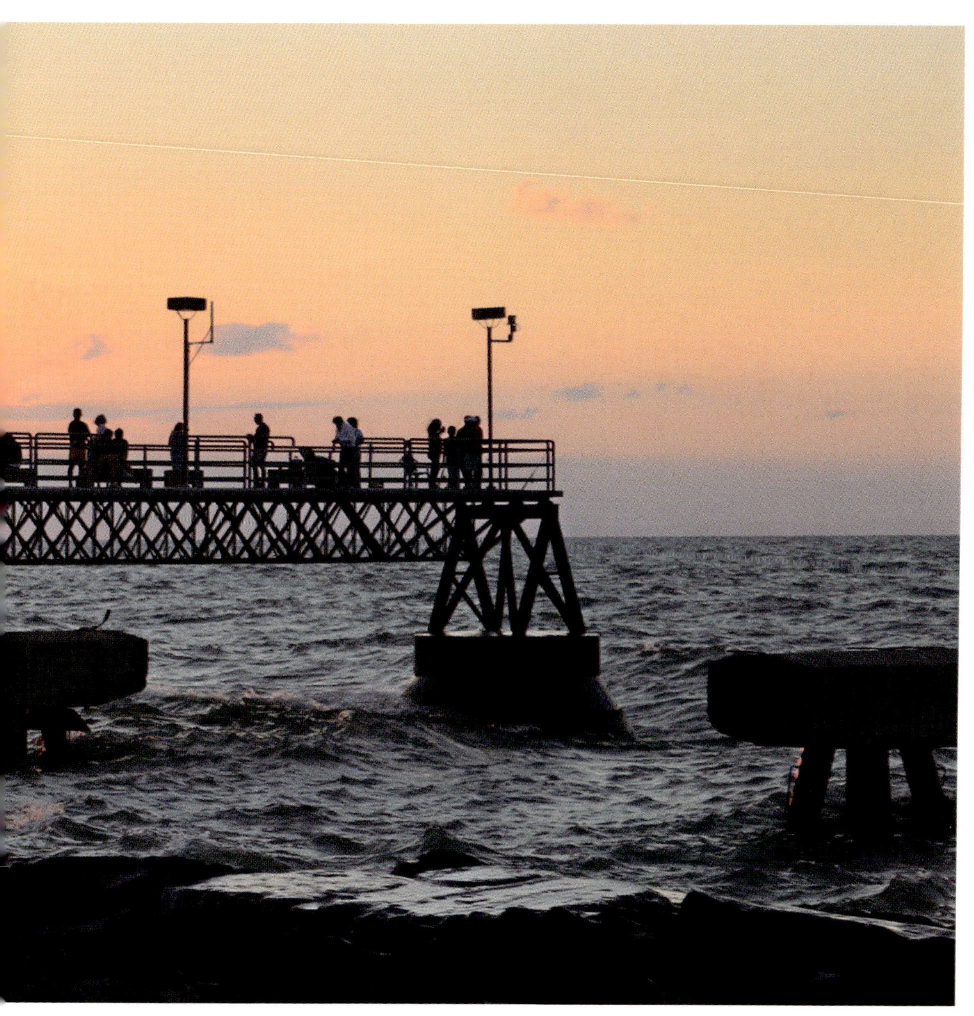

The sun sets over Edgewater Fishing Pier in Edgewater Park.

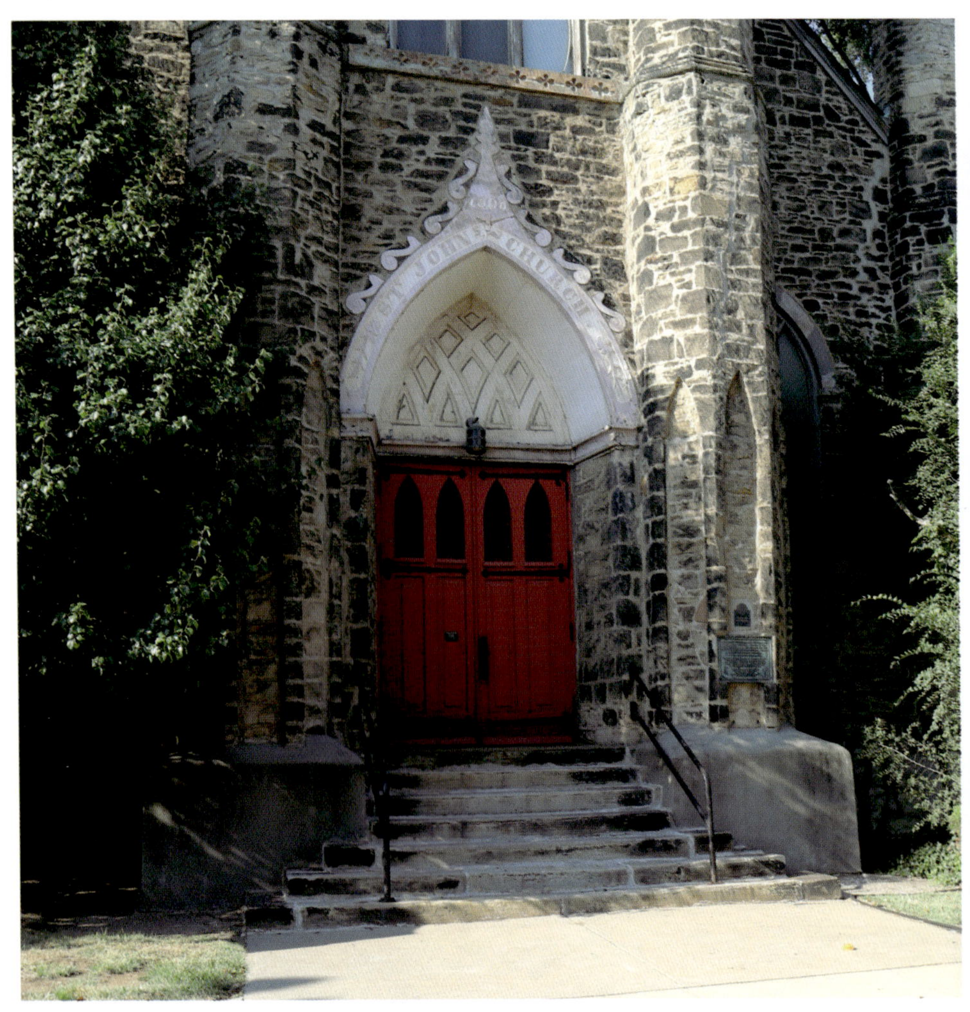

St. John's Church in Ohio City was a key point on the Underground Railroad.

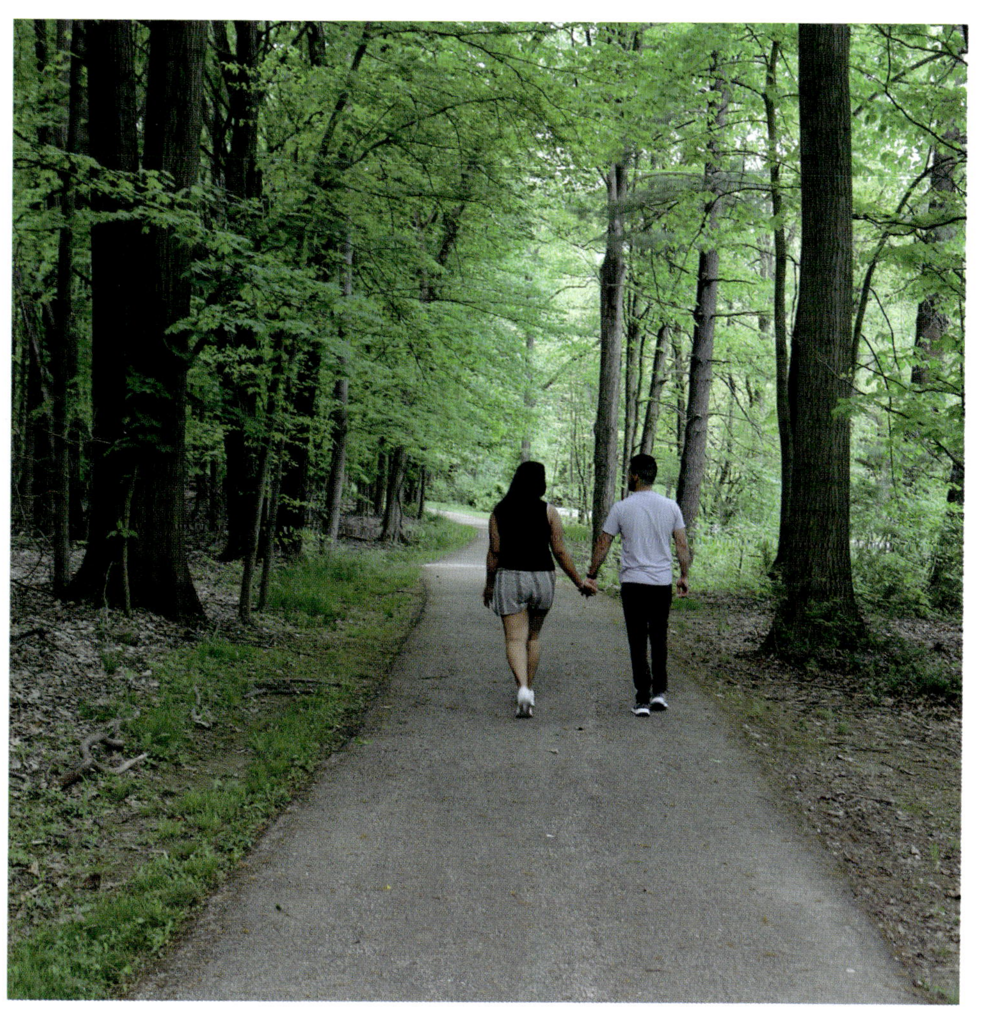

A walk through the Cleveland Metroparks is always a delight!

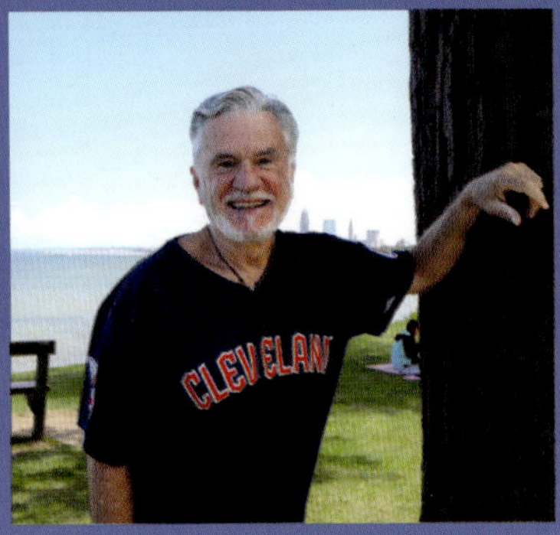

Gary J. Sikorski is a freelance photographer who has traveled extensively and photographed virtually every country in western Europe, as well as parts of South America, Mexico, the Caribbean, and several islands in Hawaii. He currently resides in Cleveland and is the author of a number of photographic books.

Other Schiffer Books by the Author:
101 Things to Do in Cleveland, 978-0-7643-7023-6
101 Things to Do in Key West, 978-0-7643-5476-2
101 Things to Do in Rhode Island, 978-0-7643-5138-9
101 Things to Do in Martha's Vineyard, 978-0-7643-4953-9

Library of Congress Control Number: 2025941570

Designed by Alexa Harris
Cover design by Molly Shields
Type set in Roboto

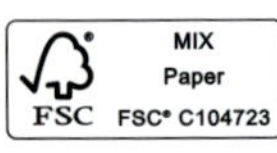

ISBN: 978-0-7643-7115-8
ePub: 978-1-5073-0674-1

Printed in China

10 9 8 7 6 5 4 3 2 1

Published by Schiffer Publishing, Ltd.
4880 Lower Valley Road
Atglen, PA 19310
Phone: (610) 593-1777; Fax: (610) 593-2002
Email: info@schifferbooks.com
Web: www.schifferbooks.com

For our complete selection of fine books on this and related subjects, please visit our website at www.schifferbooks.com. You may also write for a free catalog.

Schiffer Publishing's titles are available at special discounts for bulk purchases for sales promotions or premiums. Special editions, including personalized covers, corporate imprints, and excerpts, can be created in large quantities for special needs. For more information, contact the publisher.

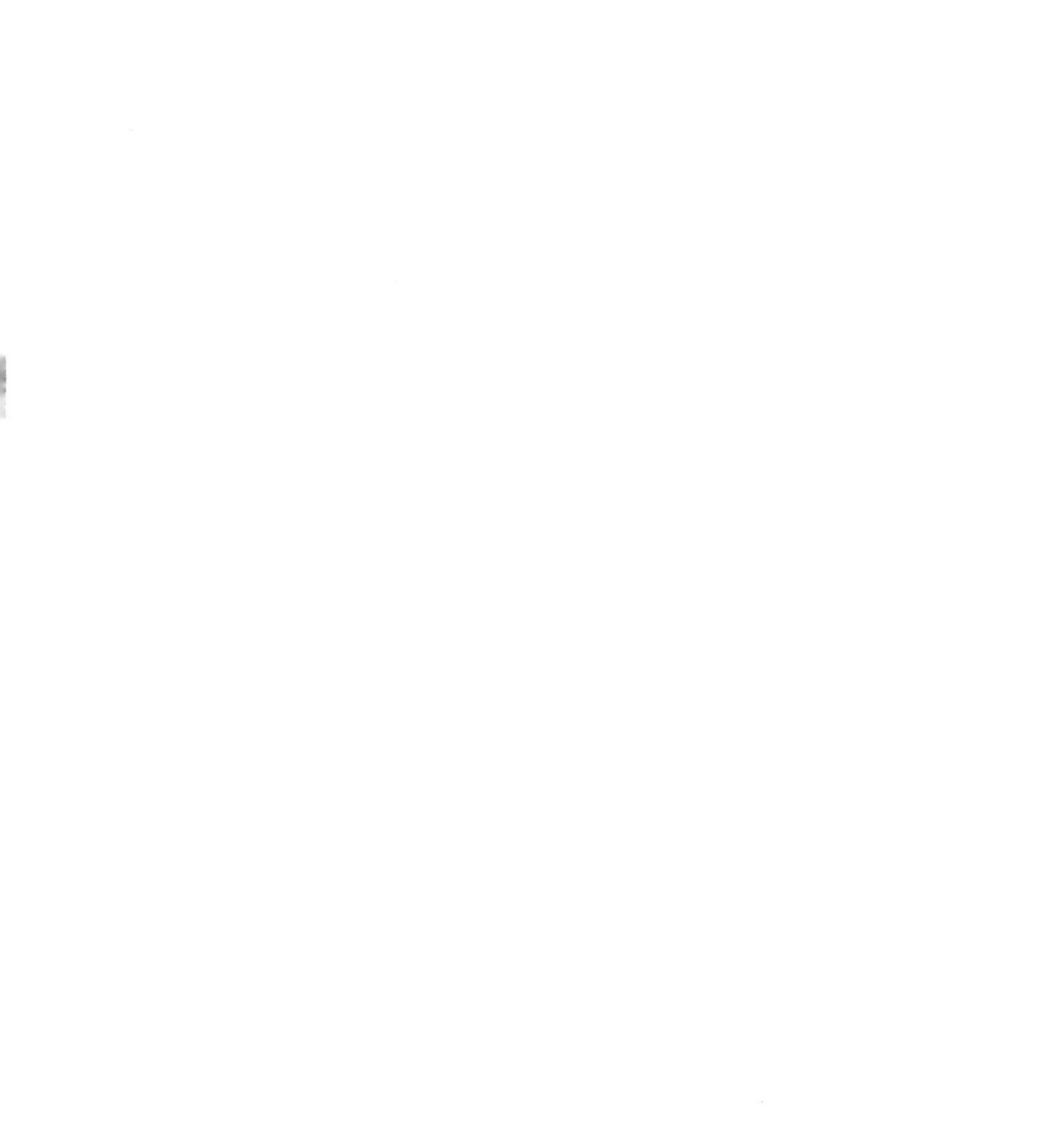